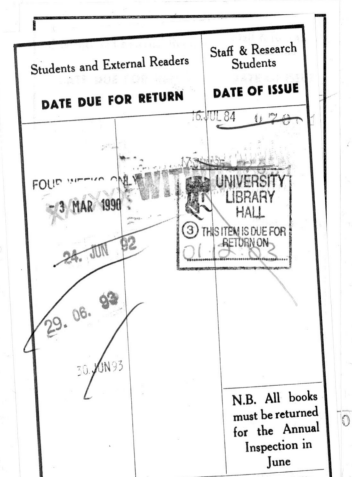

Community Work and Social Change

Community Work
and Social Change

THE REPORT OF A STUDY GROUP ON TRAINING
SET UP BY THE
CALOUSTE GULBENKIAN FOUNDATION
CHAIRMAN
EILEEN YOUNGHUSBAND, D.B.E.

Longmans

LONGMANS, GREEN AND CO LTD
London and Harlow

Associated companies, branches and representatives
throughout the world

© Longmans, Green & Co Ltd 1968
First published 1968

0582 428602

Set in Monotype Times
and printed in Great Britain by
The Camelot Press Ltd, London and Southampton

Foreword

In April 1965 a number of people interested in community work approached the Calouste Gulbenkian Foundation through its London Branch with the suggestion that a small *ad hoc* committee should be invited to examine the possibility of convening a representative conference on training for community work in the United Kingdom. Discussion of this proposal led to the abandonment of the idea of a conference, in favour of an enquiry into the nature and extent of community work with a view to making proposals for training. The Foundation gladly undertook to sponsor the work of a Study Group formed for this purpose. With the agreement of the members of the Group, the Foundation asked Dame Eileen Younghusband to act as Chairman. Her consent to this proposal was thus at the outset a piece of great good fortune.

The moment was opportune for such a move, for the growing interest and participation in community work among professional social workers, adult educationalists, members of voluntary organisations, local councillors, social planners, and others were beginning to be reflected in an increasing awareness of the need for appropriate training. It was also clear that these developments would be relevant to much current investigation, such as that of the Seebohm Committee and the Royal Commissions on Local Government in England and Scotland.

The present book is the result of over two years' work. It is right that it should be prefaced by an expression of appreciation on the part of the Foundation for the time, thought and care which have been so ungrudgingly devoted to its compilation. The book could not have been written without the wide range of knowledge and experience which Dame Eileen and the members of the Group individually and collectively have brought to bear upon it. In thanking them, the Trustees of the Foundation wish also, on behalf of the Study Group and on their own behalf, to thank a number of other people who allowed themselves to be called upon for help and advice as occasion arose. The published work owes much not only to the social scientists who are mentioned in the course of the book, but in particular, to the contribution from Mr Peter Leonard. Also, during the last six months of its labours the Study Group benefited greatly from the collaboration of Professor Robert Perlman of the Community Organisation Curriculum Development Project at Brandeis University, Massachusetts. The help which he and others gave was not only valuable in itself as a direct contribution to the work but was also an encouragement by implying recognition by those in the community and social work world of the need for the work to be done, and to be done well.

The Foundation invited the members of the Study Group in their personal capacity, and none of the views expressed in the following pages is to be taken as representing any of the organisations with which individual members of the Group may be associated. If, as a result of their joint task, the discussion of community work in the context of social planning is taken a stage further, giving rise to well-planned experiment in training for community work, those who have contributed to the work of the Study Group will be well pleased, and the Foundation will fully share their satisfaction.

José de Azeredo Perdigão,
Chairman,
The Calouste Gulbenkian Foundation,
Lisbon.

Contents

and the individual; values related to practice; professional ethics; the community worker's own values; the limitations of self-determination; who knows best?

Part Three: Training

Priorities and the need for a coherent pattern of training; professional training for full time community work; an organisational pattern for professional training in community work; the qualifying award; selection; teaching staff; courses for members of related professions with a community work function; in-service training; evaluation.

A basis for selection; problems of selecting material from the social sciences; the importance of developing a theory of practice; a framework for curriculum planning; the contribution of the social sciences: the contribution of psychology; the contribution of sociology; the contribution of economics and social history; methods of social investigation; the contribution of politics, government and social administration; the importance of social philosophy; American experience; conclusions.

Criteria for planning specific courses; training objectives; methods of teaching the social sciences; principles and methods of community work; teaching community work in relation to specific social problems; various methods of presentation and study.

The purpose of fieldwork; observation and study of community situations; the range of field experience; patterns of field experience; agencies for supervised field practice; fieldwork teachers; selection of fieldwork; the students' fieldwork experience;

reports on students' fieldwork; length and type of placement; possible developments; assessment of students' total performance in the theory and practice elements of the course.

Part Four: Conclusions

The need for coordinated planning; financial implications of training programmes; the need for a national council to promote training for community work; a strategy for the use of scarce teaching resources.

Appendices

Members of the Study Group on Training for Community Work

1966–1968

Dame Eileen Younghusband, D.B.E., J.P. (Chairman)	Adviser on Social Work Training, National Institute for Social Work Training until March 1967.
Dr T. R. Batten	Reader in Community Development Studies, University of London Institute of Education.
Mr J. Hywel Griffiths	Lecturer in Community Development, Department of Adult Education, University of Manchester.
Mr Peter Hodge	Lecturer in Social Administration, Department of Social Science and Social Administration, London School of Economics.
Mr David Jones, O.B.E.	Senior Lecturer, Community Social Work, National Institute for Social Work Training.
Mr R. A. B. Leaper (from February 1967)	Lecturer in Social Administration, Department of Social Administration, University College of Swansea.
Miss Elisabeth Littlejohn, J.P.	Secretary, Standing Conference of Councils of Social Service, National Council of Social Service.
Mr A. V. S. Lochhead	Director of Social Administration Courses, University College of Swansea.
Mr Richard Mills	Deputy Director, United Kingdom and British Commonwealth Branch, Calouste Gulbenkian Foundation.
Mrs Muriel Smith, M.B.E.	Community Development Officer, London Council of Social Service.
Dr D. F. Swift	Tutor in Sociology, Oxford University Department of Education.
Professor E. A. O. G. Wedell	Professor of Adult Education, University of Manchester.
Professor Roger Wilson, J.P. (absent in the United States from January 1968)	Professor of Education and Social Development, Department and Institute of Education, University of Bristol.

Mr R. C. Wright — Chief Professional Adviser, Council for Training in Social Work.

Miss Lesley Sewell, O.B.E. (Administrative Officer from January 1967) — Formerly General Secretary, National Association of Youth Clubs.

Acknowledgements

No report is produced without much hard work both by its authors and those behind the scenes. As chairman and editor I have had good reason to experience the unfailing help of J. C. Thornton, Director of the United Kingdom and British Commonwealth Branch of the Calouste Gulbenkian Foundation; the support, wisdom and wide knowledge of Richard Mills; and of Lesley Sewell whose experience and administrative ability came when it was most needed. Also of Shirley Knight who typed, retyped, checked and rechecked and, best of all, thought accuracy important; and of the duplicating and other staff at the Gulbenkian Foundation's London Branch, who with good humour and efficiency bore with our invasion. The Study Group wishes to record its indebtedness to all of them for their help in discharging the task with which the Foundation entrusted it.

EILEEN YOUNGHUSBAND
Chairman.

May 1968

question for community work is whether organisational structures can be devised and people trained and employed to facilitate citizen participation and to make it more effective, as well as making public and voluntary services more acceptable and usable. In short, community work is a means of giving life to local democracy.

THE REPORT AND ITS READERS

In this report we raise some of the many issues in community work. We hope that these and our proposals in relation to some of them will be discussed by various groups with a view to action. The Seebohm Committee[1] and the Royal Commissions on Local Government for England and Scotland had not finished their work when the present report went to press but they are likely to cover similar issues from different angles.

We hope that this report will be read by administrators, community workers, social workers, the clergy, teachers, youth leaders and others, including some overseas readers. Some of these readers may say we have made the simple complicated and overstated the obvious; others that sometimes what we have left out is more relevant than what we include. This is inevitable in writing for a diverse audience, and when the subject itself is many sided, with fluid boundaries and not yet capable of clear definition. What matters is not that this report should propose so-called definitive statements but that it should stimulate discussion about important social issues.

The detailed table of contents will guide different readers to the sections of most interest to them but it is necessary to read the whole report to see the interrelation of the different parts.

---

[1] Its Report was published in July, 1968. It argues that 'a general responsibility for community development . . . must become an essential part of the work of the social service department' (para 484) and emphasises the importance of citizen participation. It also proposes that designated social development areas should receive extra resources and comprehensive planning. All social service departments should have a senior staff member responsible for community work planning and consultation. The field staff should engage in community work. 'Universities should accept a major responsibility for experiment and development in . . . training for social work with communities . . .' (para 545). Generic training should 'equip students to work as appropriate with individuals, groups or communities' (para 558). There should be 'opportunities to develop skills to a higher level in subsequent training' (para 560). A single advisory council should be set up with a training committee responsible for all forms of social work training.

PART ONE

The Current Situation

2

Trends and Growing Points

This chapter deals with some of the reasons which have led to discussions about community action and community work. There is no intention to do more than illustrate these, and some important aspects are not covered, for instance human relations in industrial or other functional communities, or the particular problems of rural areas. If certain principles emerge it is likely that these would apply to some extent no matter what the setting.

REASONS FOR THE GROWTH OF INTEREST IN COMMUNITY WORK

The intensified growth in economic, social and geographical mobility accelerated by the Second World War and its aftermath has created or made manifest new needs in the community field different from and on a larger scale than those with which the early community planners and workers had to deal. This new interest in community work has many strands. These may be conveniently viewed from three angles: *Situations whose impact on people is clarifying a need for community work* include the movement of large numbers of people to new towns or new housing estates which creates a whole range of community needs and potential tensions which demand action. There are multiple problems in some twilight areas where depressed minorities suffer from bad housing, poor schools and a debilitating physical and social environment. There is a need here to evoke community response as part of a comprehensive plan for improvement.

The rapid mobility of populations in many urban areas and the presence of substantial minority groups give rise to frustration, to conflict and to a high incidence of family difficulty. Community work appears to provide one method of tackling some of these problems.

The effects of some of these situations in terms of social change and its consequences for people. These changes mean that because of specialisation, diversity and mobility, and because of physical features of urban living, the kind of community life which traditionally was based on a neighbourhood is rare.

The accelerating rate of social change is experienced by people as a result of occupational, status and geographical mobility with their consequences for family life and social relationships. 'This frees people from what they do not like. But it leaves them on their own to discover what they do like and enjoy and value.'[1] This may create difficulties of adjustment and of forming a close association with other people. A related feature of this rapid change and mobility is that most individuals play various roles which are often determined by external agencies and related to a succession of different people, not only over long periods but within a single day or week.

Paradoxically, in a large and complex society, the individual's choice is simultaneously extended and restricted. 'He wants the security that only large-scale social organisation can afford but at the same time he craves the ability to shape at least a part of his own destiny.'[2] These opposing tensions have not anywhere been reconciled and it is not only the hidden persuaders of the commercial world, but also the scale of central and local government, of industry and the social services that limit opportunities for active participation and decision. The grass roots of democracy often languish in consequence.

The need in community planning to think in terms of whole persons and of the satisfaction of their needs as persons in social interaction with each other, rather than focus attention on a series of separate needs and problems. This suggests that community work as an approach to people's social needs has its necessary counterpart in an integrated approach to planning and administration at national, regional and local levels.

The many specialised divisions of expanding statutory and voluntary social services raise problems of overlapping, of conflicting aims, of confusion to the administrator and public alike. This focuses attention on the need for coordination in the interests of planning for people rather than concentrating upon a series of symptoms in isolation from each other.

Administrators are increasingly aware of the difficulties which large-scale organisations have in maintaining good relations with the public they serve. Community work has a part to play in making their services better understood and enabling organisations themselves to be more sensitive to the needs, wishes and discontents of the consumers of public services. The increasing scale and complexity of administrative, economic, technological and political structures emphasises the need for such an understanding. Technology tends to make life less immediate and personal; decision is remote from the individual; the technicalities which govern organisations are beyond his comprehension; he is bound by rules not of his making and indeed outside his competence to make or modify. The new town

1. Roger Wilson, *Difficult Housing Estates*, Tavistock Publications, London, 1963, p. 11.
2. Elizabeth Wickenden, 'What are the social priorities for the modern city?', in *Urban Development: its Implications for Social Welfare*, Proceedings of the XIIIth International Conference of Social Work, Washington, D.C., 1966, p. 126.

in which he lives, the factory in which he works, the political party for which he votes, the education system which serves his children, the hospital his wife attends, may each be such an organisation. At what point does he break in and have his say and make his contribution? In what ways is it appropriate and desirable that he should do so?

In more specific fields of work such as adult education, youth work and the relationships between school and home, community work offers a new and possibly useful approach. In addition, social caseworkers find in much of their work, whether child care, social work with the elderly, handicapped or mentally ill, long-term support for ex-prisoners, or with minority groups, that they are in fact having to undertake community work in order to mobilise local resources, concern and action. No matter where it is practised, this approach aims to stimulate greater participation by and greater sensitivity towards the people served. Indeed to foster action by citizens for the improvement of their own communities is an important objective in its own right.

In the rest of this chapter we first describe some current and evolving trends towards integrated planning and the relationship of these trends to community work in the field. Later, from p. 14 to p. 25, recent developments and growing points are considered in relation to the role of community work in various services of social and educational significance. Finally, this leads on in the next chapter to an analysis of community work and community workers which will provide a basis for the rest of the report.

THE EVOLUTION OF COMMUNITY ORGANISATION AND COMMUNITY DEVELOPMENT OVERSEAS

Community organisation and community development as they have evolved in other countries have affected developments here. In most parts of the world the growth of mobility and the rapidity of change have created a need for more explicit forms of social and communal organisation. In the U.S.A. community organisation has come to be identified, alongside casework and group work, as one of the three methods of social work.[1] We also refer to this in more detail in chapter 10.

Until very recently community development has been mainly associated with attempts to solve the problems encountered by emergent rural peoples in the developing countries, or in such relatively underdeveloped areas of their countries as southern Italy, Sicily, and the Indian reservations in Canada and the United States. Much of its rationale owes a debt to the voluntary self-help activities

1. See appendix B for a fuller note on community organisation and community development.

in nineteenth- and early twentieth-century Britain. This experience was used extensively in the encouragement of social action in many of the former British colonial territories, and adapted to the needs of the developing countries of Africa and Asia. In the course of this adaptation a good deal has been learned about the processes of community development, both in rural and urban conditions, and links have also been forged with community organisation. Inevitably community work is deeply affected by local people's attitudes and values. None the less some concepts are universal and much that has been discovered elsewhere is applicable to community work in this country.

MOVES TOWARDS AN INTEGRATIVE APPROACH IN SOCIAL POLICY

The need for an integrated approach in social policy, recognised in recent years, has led to a growth of interest in community-oriented activities. The considerable expansion and refinement of sociology and psychology in the last twenty-five years or so is beginning to provide a conceptual key to the understanding of community dysfunction which was not available before. This has now begun to make available tools for the systematic planning of an environment favourable to the growth of social relations.

The change in the role of government from the regulative to the dynamic has produced such positive social policy interventions as the social security scheme, the national health service, the provision of free secondary education for all, the child care service, and housing and town and country planning legislation. The operation of these separate services has demonstrated their interrelations from the point of view of people's needs and thus the urgency of devising common policies between them. Governments of both political parties have begun to recognise that development policies involve the close interplay of social and economic factors and that only integrated planning for social development can prevent imbalances that result in success in one sector and failure in another.

The purpose of community work is not only to promote better all round coordination, but also to press for action to protect the interests of groups with special needs. These include, amongst others, such diverse needs as those of unsupported mothers and their children, housebound mothers with children under five, spastics and alienated young people. Some of these groups are more socially acceptable than others; in some instances to advocate that scarce resources should be diverted to meet their needs may arouse local good will but in others hostility.

A striking example of the need to see the interrelation of social and economic policies has been provided by the work of the Regional

Economic Advisory Councils and the Regional Economic Planning Boards which were established early in 1965. The objective of government was to stimulate economic development in the regions. As one council after another has produced its analysis of the needs of its region it has pointed to the inevitable link between economic viability and social health, defined in terms of housing, environmental factors, and the educational and cultural infrastructure which makes a human zone attractive to its actual and potential residents. The councils and boards have therefore found themselves having to consider both primary and secondary causes of economic stagnation. They have been faced with the results of underinvestment in the social and cultural sectors over a period of several generations. Accordingly they are having to address themselves to the promotion of development on a broad front. Higher productivity requires not only investment in new machinery but also the provision of a housing and cultural and physical environment which attracts and retains the more able workers.

Recognition at this level of the need for an integrated approach to development is new. No formal provision was made in the original structure of either the councils or the boards for the necessary terms of reference. These bodies have had to find out the gaps in their equipment by trial and error. Clearly their work would have been a good deal easier if their broader role had been recognised from the outset. At the same time the unanimity with which the councils have discovered, independently of each other, that their exclusively economic brief is inadequate, is a telling confirmation of the truism that planning is for people.

NEW APPROACHES IN ORGANISATION

The concept of community intervention has significant consequences for social work, and for social development services and planning. Given the process of interaction between environment, social phenomena, and social provision; given also the consequences of accelerating social change, comprehensive social planning is essential. Evidence of this is to be found in national and regional planning, in new town development corporations, in the coordinating activities of councils of social service, in the criticisms of the lack of effective coordination in some social services, and in the Report of the Maud Committee, which recommends substantial changes in the present organisation and administration of local government.[1]

The participation of social scientists and social workers in planning is necessary so that the human consequences of technological change may be given their proper weight together with physical and

1. *Report of the Committee on Management of Local Government*, vol. I, H.M.S.O., 1967 (hereafter cited as *Management of Local Government*).

economic consequences. An outstanding example is the continuing influence of housing policies and housing shortages on community work. Planning that closely affects people's lives should include interaction with them, through consultation or direct involvement. If problems are to be correctly analysed, and action taken which is relevant to the needs of local people in general or of particular groups and within the resources of the community it is necessary to take account of local people's views about what they want most.

In an increasingly well-educated democracy, influenced by the mass media, the demand that those who use services should have a say in their operation is often nullified by growth in size and complexity which makes it less and less possible for the man in the street to exercise an informed judgement about such matters as the siting of airports, or whether schools should 'go comprehensive'. To press people to assume responsibilities beyond their powers creates disillusionment; but it is essential that they should exercise these capacities up to the limit if local democracy is to have meaning. Much local community action is in practice undertaken by local councillors, and by members of innumerable voluntary organisations, including the churches. There are also significant moves at present for consumers of a service to demand more power, through parent–teacher associations, tenants' associations, associations of hospital patients and the like.

PROBLEMS AND GROWING POINTS

Problems and growing points in the civil service

The Osmond Report[1] recommended three stages in the career of those with management responsibilities in the civil service at which the training arrangements should include study of the social content of administrative work undertaken by central government departments. The twenty-week course which all assistant principals at present attend in their third year of service provides little opportunity for a social bias. It is mainly concerned with questions of economic policy, although the economic aspects of social policy (studies of health, education, poverty and unemployment) figure marginally in the curriculum. Therefore the Osmond Report envisaged the introduction of a further course, also of twenty weeks' duration, which would be attended by assistant principals at a point when they were approaching promotion. And it recommended that the syllabus for this second course should include an introduction to social administration.

At the middle management level (principal or equivalent rank in the other classes) a second stage of in-service training provides at the

1. *Report of the Working Party on Management Training in the Civil Service*, H.M.S.O., 1967.

14

present time for a linked series of four courses lasting between three and six weeks each. One of these is concerned with social administration. At the third stage, senior officers of assistant secretary and equivalent rank attend short seminars on specific subjects related to their interests or more immediate responsibilities. It has to be recognised, however, that the scale of the provision thus envisaged is not large.

It is to be hoped that the Royal Commission on the Civil Service[1] will recognise the need to include in future training arrangements not merely studies of the social services but also studies directed to a much broader appreciation of the community perspective implicit, for good or ill, in a wide range of government decisions which appear to have no overt connection with the quality of life of the local community. In short, national studies of social development should be kept in balance with economic studies and attempts made to remedy the curious lack which there seems to be at present of material to help administrators to understand social structure and social relationships. Furthermore, it is important that such studies should extend beyond the social service departments properly so called and should be undertaken also by those in economic departments whose decisions have social implications and consequences. Lastly, it is desirable that civil service training schemes should be on a scale large enough to include all officers in the relevant grades.

There has been a trend in recent years for the inspectorates of various government departments to become more concerned with advisory than regulative functions. For instance in the White Paper on *Children in Trouble* it is envisaged that 'inspectors will take part in the work of Joint Planning Committees and will form a link between the Home Office, local authorities and voluntary organisations as part of the cooperative effort to foster the spread of new knowledge and techniques in the care of children'.[2]

Problems and growing points in local government
The fact that much of the quality of life in a local community depends on its local government emphasises the importance of a thorough understanding of the community perspective both by the elected members of local authorities and by their officials. The Maud[3] and Mallaby[4] reports have recommended action to improve the standard of local government in this and other respects.[5] On the grounds of efficiency the Maud Committee recommended larger

1. The report was not available when this report went to press.
2. *Children in Trouble*, H.M.S.O., 1968, p. 16.
3. *Management of Local Government*, vol. 1.
4. Report of the Committee, *Staffing of Local Government*, H.M.S.O., 1967.
5. The reports of the Royal Commissions on Local Government were not available when this report went to press.

units and regional planning. There will certainly be a place for community policy and planning officers in such a structure. The Committee was equally concerned that the opportunities for active citizen participation should not be smothered in large bureaucratic structures and that local council members should be equipped to perform their appropriate functions. In the study of *The Local Government Councillor* undertaken for the Committee it was found that only 15 per cent of councillors (compared with 53 per cent of members of Parliament) had had further or higher education.[1] In view of the growing complexity of much local government work the Committee feared that this would lead to a widening gulf between the expertise of the professional officers and the limitations of the laymen. It is interesting to note that here, as in much writing on the subject at the present time, the community aspect is implicit rather than explicit, largely because the need for a body of knowledge in this field is sensed but not yet articulate. The need to bring this into the open is the more urgent since the Committee's study shows councillors to be heavily engaged in other local organisations concerned with religious, welfare, community and leisure activities. Eighty-eight per cent of the sample were members of one or more such organisations; 44 per cent being members of between four and seven of these. And 'more than half of all the organisations to which councillors belong were concerned with educational, religious, welfare or leisure purposes'.[2] Clearly, council members have a crucial function in community organisation and social planning, though they are circumscribed by limitations of time and expertise.

The range of local authority officials who in one way or another affect the wellbeing of the community is exceptionally wide. Among professional staff so concerned are not only child care officers, mental welfare officers, social welfare officers, psychiatric and medical social workers, doctors, nurses, education officers, teachers, youth organisers, health inspectors, health visitors and others, but also architects, planning officers, civil and municipal engineers and building inspectors. A number of recent and relevant official and other enquiries on the services dealing with children and young people include: the Ingleby[3] and Kilbrandon[4] Reports and the Scottish and English White Papers.[5]

Social work has largely grown around a casework function in helping individuals with social or personal difficulties, but three new general trends are brought out in these and other reports.

The first is a shift in practice and thinking towards considering the

1. The Maud Report, vol. 2, Table 1.14, p. 27.
2. *Ibid.*, vol. 2, Table 6.1, pp. 184–5.
3. *The Committee on Children and Young Persons*, H.M.S.O., 1960.
4. *The Committee on Children and Young Persons* (Scotland), H.M.S.O., 1964.
5. The White Paper on *Social Work and the Community* (Scotland), H.M.S.O., 1967, the White Paper on *Children in Trouble*, H.M.S.O., 1968.

individual in relation to his family and to the wider social network. This has led to the increasing use of group work methods, and attempts at prevention and long-term social support. It is already clear that there is a community work element in the day-to-day activities of a large number of staff hitherto thought of as caseworkers only. This particularly applies to those engaged in community care and after-care, and in preventive services for children. There is a related emphasis on interaction in administrative work at head office or district level. Separate officers are in some cases being appointed to deal with coordination.

The second trend is to examine more fully the cultural and environmental factors in social dysfunction and to attempt to deal with both these and the psychological factors in a particular case. The concepts of social therapy, social education and community action are consequences of growing psychological and sociological problem analysis.

The third trend is to reconsider the whole administrative structure of the personal social services so that better coordination may be possible in the interests of the consumer and of efficiency. This is the primary task of the Seebohm Committee. Scotland will take a significant step in this direction when the new social work departments are set up under the Social Work (Scotland) Act 1968 to bring together the social work functions in different local authority departments and the probation service. This, together with the Social Work Services Group with its social work advisers in the Scottish Home and Health Department, should increase the likelihood of community planning. The joint planning committees envisaged in the White Paper on *Children in Trouble* are also significant since these would cross departmental, local government and voluntary organisation boundaries in joint planning of certain services for children.

The tone of a particular local authority is set by its clerk and by his lay or professional administrative colleagues. In recent years there has been a move towards the recognition of the clerk as a manager rather than as primarily the local authority's legal adviser, and one or two major authorities have appointed managers. But in these appointments the emphasis has been on managerial ability rather than on the official's competence and understanding of the community aspects of his job. Both are necessary if the functional approach to community work is to be realised. The Mallaby Committee recommended that: 'There should be a greater emphasis on administrative and social matters in the training of those solicitors who propose to follow a career in local government or other branches of the public service beyond the present optional paper in the Law Society's Final Examination.'[1]

Among the Committee's extensive recommendations for the

1. *The Staffing of Local Government*, para 212(a) (ii), p. 70.

training of other local authority staff[1] there is surprisingly little recognition of training needs beyond those relating to the various specialisms. This also seems to apply to the recommendations of the Royal Commission on Medical Education about training in community medicine.[2] It seems to us essential, in a situation in which local authority services have a strong tendency to operate in isolation from each other, for all officials to have, as part of their training, a substantial area of common study of the social conditions in which they operate, and how public intervention in one field of activity affects others. Indeed there exists an 'important need for cooperation at policy making and management levels, in the improvement and promotion of measures which would help both to prevent the occurrence of . . . problems and to enable communities and individuals more readily to surmount problems and resolve tensions by their own efforts'.[3]

Problems and growing points in new communities

The general needs of local communities for competent and imaginative elected representatives and officials are felt in any local situation, however well-established and stable. Where a community is new, or has to undergo the upheaval of extensive urban renewal with consequent population transfers, the need for persons competent to undertake effective community organisation and social planning is even greater. Their task is to plan the environment in such a way that uprooted people can be resettled with the minimum disruption of their social relationships, and to encourage the formation of organisations through which residents can participate in providing adequate expression for their community life.[4] How life looks to the rehoused families will determine whether local leadership and communal activities begin to grow.

Social facilities in new communities were explored by a subcommittee of the Central Housing Advisory Committee of the Ministry of Housing and Local Government.[5] The Committee's recommendations on staffing cover a range of posts concerned with the development of community institutions and agencies. They emphasise the need for a responsible director or manager of town development, and recall the recommendations of an earlier report,[6] 'that an "Arrivals Officer" should be appointed or nominated to

1. *Ibid.*, pp. 163–6.
2. *Report of the Royal Commission on Medical Education*, H.M.S.O., 1968, pp. 66–9 and 115 (the section on the behavioural sciences, pp. 104–9, relates to undergraduate medical courses).
3. *Social Work and the Community*, pp. 4–5.
4. See J. H. Nicholson, *New Communities in Britain*, National Council of Social Service, 1961.
5. *The Needs of New Communities*, H.M.S.O., 1967, p. 1.
6. *The First Hundred Families*, H.M.S.O., 1965.

act as "the friend and adviser" of newcomers'. The Committee endorse this recommendation and add: 'The question of the Department to which the Arrivals Officer should be attached is of much less importance than the clear principle that there ought to be one ... it is important that he should have the necessary skills for the job and that he is adequately relieved of his existing duties.'[1]

The Committee also recommend the extension to expanding towns of the practice in new towns of appointing a social relations officer. They point out that such an appointment is also appropriate to major rehousing areas in existing towns.

Problems and growing points in twilight areas

There would seem to be no reason, other than the Committee's terms of reference, why the proposal above should be limited to new housing. The claims of slums in course of redevelopment and of twilight areas which 'will inevitably remain for many years to come'[2] are at least as urgent. The people in these areas of housing stress are 'those with the lowest incomes, those with average incomes and large families and many of the newcomers to London'.[3] Here 'all kinds of problems become "clotted" and entangled with one another'.[4]

The Milner Holland Committee suggested 'that areas in which bad housing is concentrated should be designated as areas of special control in which bad living conditions would be attacked comprehensively, assisted by an enlargement of powers'.[5] This proposal has been reiterated by the National Committee for Commonwealth Immigrants who point out that 'it is not possible to consider an area of special housing need without considering deficiencies in all other social services that exist within such an area, and the need to rehabilitate these services at the same time as examining housing problems', and they go on to say that 'unless the problems of "areas of special housing need" are treated patiently and helpfully, and members of the public at large (in addition to those who actually are in such areas) given every opportunity to understand the steps which are being taken, the solution may well introduce problems almost as serious as those which are being alleviated'.[6]

Professor Rex comments that 'there is no special provision for community services, other than through grants to community centres, which are thought of too often in suburban terms. What is

1. *The Needs of New Communities*, paras 202 and 203.
2. *Report of the Committee on Housing in Greater London* (the Milner Holland Report), H.M.S.O., 1965, p. 122.
3. *Ibid.*, p. 91.
4. Ruth Glass and John Westergaard, *London's Housing Needs*, Centre for Urban Studies Report No. 5, p. 46.
5. Milner Holland Report, p. 228.
6. *Areas of Special Housing Need*, National Committee for Commonwealth Immigrants, London, 1967.

necessary is a restructuring of these services so as to make the kind of services which Sparkbrook has so painfully acquired universal in the twilight zones.'[1] He suggests that: 'the leaders of the various ethnic, class and other groups should meet regularly to define common interests and to find peaceful compromises where there were conflicts of interest. This is the work of community associations in zones of transition. . . . The central problem is that there should be sufficient detached individuals willing to give the necessary time to playing a mediating role.'[2] These proposals overlap with the Plowden Committee's[3] recommendations concerning comprehensive planning and positive discrimination in relation to education priority areas (see p. 23).

Problems and growing points in settlements and community and neighbourhood centres

Some settlements have faced an apparent decline in their relevance to contemporary needs and in the effectiveness of their work. In others there have been remarkable signs of growth and innovation, particularly when combined with imaginative use of resources from trusts and foundations and in achieving better relationships than ever before with local authorities. In part, settlements fill the role of neighbourhood centres, continuing their traditional method of sponsoring and supporting clubs for the young and old. Nearly all settlements are still residential centres and, at their best, the residents offer valuable help to settlement programmes while themselves learning something of the social circumstances of the locality, through their commitment to work in it. Grouping settlements together in 'federations', where they are reasonably contiguous, offers opportunities for the sharing of common services and the mutual support of new work made possible by the pooling of certain resources. Further growing points are found in settlements which have initiated projects beyond their own walls or their immediate locality in order to serve other localities in deprived urban areas or new centres of population in the suburbs and out-county estates. A few settlements also think it part of their function to serve particular groups, the handicapped, discharged prisoners or former hospital patients, for example.

There has been a substantial increase in the number of full time wardens of community centres in the last fifteen years. But, taking account of the long history of the community association movement and its related institutions, the rate of growth is slow. There is at present more uncertainty about the suitability of community centres

1. John Rex and Robert Moore, *Race, Community and Conflict: a Study of Sparkbrook*, Oxford University Press, 1967, p. 220.

2. *Ibid.*, p. 284.

3. Report of the Central Advisory Council for Education (England), *Children and their Primary Schools*, H.M.S.O., 1967, p. 28.

for the promotion of a sense of community than there was immediately after the war, and no significant policy statement on the subject has been made for some years, despite the fact that the need to promote recreational and informal educational activities on a communal basis is greater than ever. It can be argued that community centres and associations have failed to rise to the challenge presented on the one hand by new and expanded towns and on the other by areas of urban renewal and rural depopulation. Meanwhile government policy has been too narrowly conceived in terms of help with the provision and maintenance of community centres. Perhaps the time has come for the government to give better support to the growing number of community associations, settlements and other neighbourhood organisations who see their work much more outside the walls of their buildings than within them and are prepared to extend their traditionally educational role into areas which in the past have been considered to be social work or social development.[1]

Problems and growing points in further education
More clarity about the need for adequate community organisation and social planning has led in recent years to the progressive development by local education authorities of facilities for post-school education. Educational building has been by far the largest sector of public building for communal use since the war. It was not until the expansion of the further education building programme that the social significance of this large volume of capital investment began to be fully realised.

Its effect has been to change the focus of educational aspiration in a large number of communities throughout the country. In many areas the local grammar school is no longer the apex of educational institutions. It has been replaced by the local technical college or college of further education. This type of institution provides post-school education of various kinds and is in this respect much more interesting to the local community than the primary and secondary schools. It tends to become, both explicitly and by custom, a centre for a wide variety of community activities, if only because it can provide facilities, such as meeting rooms, halls and catering facilities which are not available elsewhere. Hence the principals of these institutions find themselves exercising functions in relation to the local community far more varied than those stated in their terms of appointment. These community functions tend also to devolve upon other members of their staffs, particularly those concerned with liberal and general studies.

In addition to the extension of this provision for vocational further

1. Perhaps on the lines of the London Borough of Camden's community play centres. We received evidence from individual wardens of community centres where obviously there was a rich variety of community participation by people of all kinds and all ages.

education, a growing number of local education authorities have begun in recent years to extend their provision in the field of entirely non-vocational further education.

The picture throughout the country is too varied to permit any generalisation. But the example of the West Riding Local Education Authority, in a scattered and difficult geographical area, is significant (see appendix C). This authority has established seventeen posts of area principal for further education throughout those parts of the county which have a multiplicity of small local communities, many of them somewhat isolated from each other. The area principal is responsible for an area institute which may cover a dozen or more smaller communities, each with its own further education centre, generally served by part time staff.

Problems and growing points in the youth service

Having developed a largely self-contained and coherent structure for the youth service, both central government and local authorities have in recent years become conscious of the need to relate the youth service more closely to the community at large. This has arisen partly from earlier maturation and the consequent tendency for young people to demand adult rights and privileges at an earlier age, and partly from the falling age of marriage and the greater economic independence of teenagers. The abolition of national service removed a watershed between youth and adulthood from the lives of young men; the rising standard of education has created an intellectual gap between the generations; while teenage affluence has given young people far wider choices in the use of leisure, coupled with greater mobility. These and other changes have led to a much wider range of provision within the youth service, including experimental work with unattached youth.

The Youth Service Development Council of the Department of Education and Science for England and Wales is currently undertaking two enquiries: one into the relationship of the youth service with the schools and the other into the integration of young people in the adult community. They are likely to conclude that the youth leader of the future will need a much stronger community orientation both in his training and practice. He may well work more closely with other workers and agencies in the community and possibly have responsibilities which are not confined to work with young people. The organisational and training implications of a 'community centred' youth service are developed at some length in two recent books.[1, 2]

1. George Goetschius and J. Tash, *Working with Unattached Youth*, Routledge & Kegan Paul, 1967.

2. George Goetschius, *Working with Community Groups*, Routledge & Kegan Paul, 1968.

The parallel body for Scotland is the Standing Consultative Council for Youth and Community Service. From its formation in 1960 it has emphasised the importance of training. The scattered populations in many rural and urban areas of Scotland have led from the outset to attempts to integrate training for youth work and community work within the same course. In Moray House College of Education, Edinburgh, in which the training originated, the teaching has been based upon principles which apply to any age group (see also chapter 5, pp. 52–3). Social work training is now associated with these courses and this, together with the new comprehensive social work departments in Scotland, may provide some of the necessary resources for community development in its wider aspects.

Problems and growing points in the schools

Several government reports have drawn attention to the educational waste which is the consequence of a poor home background and a poor social environment. These include the Crowther Report,[1] the Newsom Report[2] and, most recent, the Plowden Report and the Gittins Report.[3] The Plowden Report is the most specific in its recommendations for action outside the school. It defines as educational priority areas districts where there is a combination of poor housing, poor services, lack of educational achievement amongst the majority of adults, substantial and poorly integrated minority groups, and high school and occupational mobility. If educational improvements are to be possible, then the wider environment and social factors must be tackled by active encouragement of parent–teacher associations and other means as well as the actual curricula and standards within the schools. From the evidence of these reports there are clearly opportunities for a development of social work between the schools and the neighbourhood which would involve community work skills and methods beyond those at present envisaged for counselling in schools.[4]

Problems and growing points in self help organisations

The raising of the educational level in the community at large has brought about the emergence of a new generation of voluntary bodies concerned, in the broadest terms, with the promotion of the consumer interest or the development of cooperative enterprise in

1. Report of the Central Advisory Council for Education (England), *15–18*, vol. 1, H.M.S.O., 1960.

2. Report of the Central Advisory Council for Education (England), *Half our Future*, H.M.S.O., 1963.

3. Report of the Central Advisory Council for Education, *Children and their Primary Schools*, H.M.S.O., 1967; Report of the Central Advisory Council (Wales), H.M.S.O., 1967.

4. The Schools Council, *Counselling in Schools*, H.M.S.O., 1967.

the community. Bodies such as the Consumers' Association and the National Federation of Consumer Groups, the Confederation of Associations for the Advancement of State Education, the Pre-School Play Groups Association; groups undertaking the care of handicapped people generally, associations of parents with children suffering from a particular disability, groups interested in the quality of the hospital service and many others have provided foci for communal activities. It is interesting to note that such activities concern not only the cooperative provision of services not otherwise available, but also the exertion of corporate pressure for the improvement of standards of provision made by statutory bodies.

Joint activities arising from tenants' associations on new housing estates, residents' associations in residential suburbs, groups to run pre-school play groups and community play centres, are significant because they indicate both the range of possibilities open to voluntary effort and the points at which it requires help and assistance in order to be effective. Often all that is required is provision for learning a skill which people can then exercise in their own time and at their own expense. Courses in child development for young mothers interested in pre-school play groups and the demand for a wide range of sociology and social work courses for persons of all ages engaged in voluntary work illustrate this trend.[1]

Problems and growing points in voluntary organisations

The legion of voluntary organisations, some local, some national with or without local branches, constitute much of the web of community life and means for the exercise of democracy. Some are both democratic (i.e. directed by the membership) and open-ended. Others have been started for particular purposes by enthusiasts who then try to awaken others to a need and the merits of their particular way of meeting it. Some organisations provide a service for others. Some are formed mainly for the members' own benefit and enjoyment. They range from a group of workers at a factory running a children's party or an outing for old people to national societies formed to promote various causes.

Voluntary groups may be as informal as those at a pub or coffee bar, or as enduring with a changing membership as a church congregation. The manner in which they operate includes clubs or other meetings of all kinds for all ages and interests, outings, holidays, parties and other special occasions, conferences, deputations and

1. Other examples from the Department of Adult Education and Extra-mural Studies of the University of Liverpool are a ten week course on 'neighbourhood and community' for youth leaders, community workers and others in contact with community organisation and community development activities and also informal seminars on community development and organisation, for people who want to discuss the implications of community development for their own work.

propaganda activities. An interesting development of recent years is that of good neighbour schemes under various auspices. The development of this network of voluntary action is itself community work and also provides a means for voicing new needs or starting new projects.

Problems and growing points in the churches
The churches are significant among voluntary organisations for two reasons. First, they command a network of many men and a number of women working full time and of premises suitable for communal activities unrivalled by any other voluntary body. Second, they have in the past carried out a number of social welfare and educational activities which have since become the responsibility of the community as a whole. In the past, too, the church and the parish were the focus of much community help and people in trouble still often turn up at the door of the clergy.

In common with other voluntary bodies, many of whose activities have been taken over by statutory authorities, there has been a tendency for the churches to try to cling to these particular activities rather than to explore those new areas, such as community work, where there is as yet little statutory provision. Yet churches have extended beyond their traditional boundaries in two directions. There has been, within individual denominations, a coming together of several parishes or congregations in the same urban or rural area with a view to providing a more comprehensive service to that area. Such 'group ministries' have also been concerned to enable the several members of a team to develop their special interests or qualifications, such as youth work, teaching, care for the elderly or for delinquents, across outdated parochial boundaries. The wish to serve the local community has also caused the congregations of different denominations in a particular area to come together for joint activities. Clergy and ministers' fraternals have met to study the needs of their constituencies together. This has led to action in various sectors of community work.

Although the formal breaking down of traditional barriers and the engagement in community work takes time, there are many clergy to whom this work would be welcome if they were trained for the job and given a clearer mandate for it. This may well apply, too, to many women church workers, and indeed to many lay members. Here, then, in the churches, their congregations, their premises, and their sometimes still powerful voice in social affairs, is a significant potential source of community work.

Explorations of this kind have begun in a number of denominations in recent years. The establishment of boards or committees concerned with social responsibility has, after initial hesitation, led to a more systematic concern with those aspects of community

25

service and planning in which local churches and groups of churches can play an important part. An interesting example is the social responsibility scheme developed in the Anglican diocese of Sheffield, which aims to relate the demand for neighbourly voluntary service in the community with a supply of persons willing to give such service. Since the first scheme was initiated in one area of Sheffield in 1963, six others have been set up in other areas. By the end of 1967 most of the central districts of Sheffield were covered. The scheme operates on an interdenominational basis and provides voluntary helpers to meet requests from the following organisations: the health visiting service, home help organisers, the home nursing service, the children's department, hospitals and the Sheffield Council of Social Service.

3

The Nature of Community Work

Professor David Donnison of the London School of Economics emphasised the need 'to equip senior people . . . to act as innovators, by incorporating teaching of the right kind in existing training courses (e.g. for medical officers of health, police officers, social workers, town planners, etc.) and by running briefer courses for such people in mid-career. But it should be clear that these are designed to equip them to do their jobs better, not to create a new kind of animal.' He did not think it necessary or desirable to make a career for 'a considerable number of permanent "change agents" . . . outside the existing power structure'.[1] Professor W. J. Mackenzie of the University of Glasgow made a similar point when he wrote:

> In the last six months I have taken part in discussions about 'public administration' training for town clerks, doctors, education officers and headmasters, town and country planners, welfare officers, research scientists, policemen. The common element is that professionals in each sphere, when they reach positions of responsibility, begin to perceive the general character of their situation and its responsibilities, and to seek support. What they need is not really 'administrative training' in a formal sense, and we are therefore forced to do a great deal of rethinking. . . . I hope your Committee will apply some thought to the problems of 'the technical man as community worker'.[2]

As Professor Donnison points out, these people are, at the senior levels at least, likely to be found largely within the power structures of society, not outside it. They will, in the majority of cases, already be specialists responsible for particular areas of planning and/or administration, whether in public health, education, environmental planning, housing or the personal social services, or with general responsibilities. Normally their duties will lie entirely within one department or another, although a growing proportion of officials now have liaison with other specialisms than their own as part of their duties (see for example the posts listed in appendix C).

1. In a communication to the Study Group, 1967. The term 'change agent' was used by the Study Group at one time but dropped later.
2. In a communication to the Study Group, 1967.

Thus, whether or not these professionals need further training in their respective specialisms or in administrative procedures, they also require an understanding, in Professor Mackenzie's phrase, of the role of 'the technical man as a community worker'. This involves more than the traditional syllabus of social administration tends to cover, though it may include a good deal of it. It is an understanding of the relationship of man to his environment and to his fellow men that is needed. This will include elements of social philosophy, psychology and sociology, as well as of geography and economics. If such common understanding informed those working in different departments one of the likely consequences would be a breaking down of the rigid departmentalism which at present mars much valuable individual effort. The preconditions for the creation of such a body of understanding are identification of the relevant concepts and of the roles and functions in which their use would be appropriate.

We agree that this community function should be distributed throughout an organisation as an element in good administration and professional service. But the argument against community work as a full time professional role is open to challenge, since common experience suggests that where no category of professionally employed people is primarily committed to the exercise and development of a particular function regarded as socially desirable it is likely that it will remain subsidiary to other professional purposes. The development of casework is instructive in this respect. Undoubtedly members of any profession which helps individuals under stress need some understanding of people's feelings (whether rational or irrational) and how to help them to cope with their personal or social problems. But casework would not have reached its present level of skill in this if it had not become a full time occupation with an underpinning from the behavioural sciences and practised as a social work method. Similarly, it is arguable that community work, making conscious use of the processes that induce or retard social change, will only manifest its potential value if it is a function exercised in its own right, with a professional training that combines the best available knowledge and practice.

AN ANALYSIS OF COMMUNITY WORK

In general terms community work can be defined as a method of dealing with problems of social change. A consequence of the speed of change is that many people are jerked out of one way of life into another, perhaps more demanding, and at any rate unfamiliar. For many this means moving house or job and learning to make new relationships and get along with new groups of people. Most people are sufficiently socialised and self-reliant to achieve this but

28

there are constant risks of superficial response, life spent keeping up with the Joneses, or of withdrawal, loss of confidence, or apathy. And the very scale on which public services are provided tends to widen the gap between 'them' and 'us'. Community work is essentially about the interrelations between people and social change, how to help people and the providers of services to bring about a more comfortable 'fit' between themselves and constant change, how to survive and grow as persons in relation with others.

We do not underestimate the complexities of this kind of holistic approach to the needs of people in local communities, nor the need for social planning units to collect data and forecast the direction of social change. We are also conscious of the need for interdepartmental and inter-agency cooperation and planning, and of the extent to which organisational structure perpetuates or lessens the risk of fragmentation in meeting the needs of persons. There is also a gulf between day-to-day operations and final purposes. As the Maud Committee puts it: 'The characteristic *result* of local government action is seen in such material things as schools, houses, traffic signs and refuse-bins. But the *purpose* of such action is invariably *human happiness*. And the action itself is taken by *people* for *people*.'[1]

It is precisely at the gap between result and purpose that community work comes in to interpret to local authorities how the services appear to the consumer, what is lacking in the services themselves and the way they are provided, and thus to facilitate a mutual adaptation between people and the services.

Beyond this, local life will only flourish if there are innumerable groups of people who come together to promote purposes that seem to them important. Many such groups will get along on their own but others may need deliberate fostering, help with finding a meeting place, with running their affairs, with resources and money raising efforts, with approaches to public authorities. Part of community work is concerned with these liaison, interpreting and supporting activities. But there is also a more active function in stimulating people to meet some local need and trying to identify the leaders in a neighbourhood who could with support carry other people along with them. Fortunately there are also large numbers of people who are quite capable of making their own relationships and interests, who may play no part in organised community affairs but none the less lead happy and active lives.

We must emphasise again that this community work function is carried out by many different people but in our view the need for it and the skill it requires in modern conditions is so great that it should also be a full time professional task.

1. *Management of Local Government*, vol. 1, para. 34 (italics in original).

'GRASS ROOTS' COMMUNITY WORK

This awkward but by now common term refers to all forms of community work direct with local people. Men, teenagers and women without children tend to have leisure time interests outside the locality where they live. But women with young children, the old or the handicapped and the poor are much more circumscribed. There are other issues which concern everyone just because they are local: what kind of housing is available, what the neighbours are like, whether shopping centres and buses are convenient, what is the distance to the primary school, where the children can play in safety.

Problems of helping an existing population to come to terms with an influx of newcomers are all the more acute where there may be racial tensions too. This raises the whole issue of concentration on particular groups or better services for everyone. For example, shortages of housing and school places are general and contribute to racial tensions. There is also need for special services to help newcomers to settle in, whether they come from the West Indies or an overcrowded city, and for established residents to accept them.

The settlements and some churches pioneered neighbourhood work. Much of it goes on in many different places under various auspices. It seems to be most consistently developed at the present day, as discussion in the previous chapter has shown, in areas of rapid population growth or twilight areas.[1] To help people to adapt to the stress of new ways of living requires realistic planning for new arrivals and quick response to their many problems. It also means making it easy for small groups to form so that people may take root in the new locality as quickly as possible. As T. R. Batten puts it: 'Should not one of the prime tests – the prime test in fact – of community development be the emergence of local leaders willing to take initiative and able to exercise responsibility, and the emergence of groups, clubs, and committees which local people control and through which they act to achieve purposes of their own? In the last analysis the community worker succeeds in so far as he succeeds in making himself redundant.'[2] This is also the approach of the 'open-ended' North Kensington Family Study, a community development project in a twilight area designed to enable groups of residents to decide on action about what they regard as their most pressing needs and with the help of the community workers, to learn social skills in meeting them. Work with tenants on new housing estates is another well-known example of local community work.

Experience shows that the difficult, the deviant, the inadequate and the delinquent tend to gather together in particular streets or parts

1. See for example, Goetschius, *Working with Community Groups*.
2. T. R. Batten, *Communities and their Development*, Oxford University Press, 1957, pp. 46–7.

of housing estates, often to the scandal of conformist neighbours whose attitudes may be quite as intractable as those of the deviants. Roger Wilson has analysed the 'solids', the 'brittles' and the 'difficults', and their mutually unhelpful relations with each other, in *Difficult Housing Estates*.[1] The difficult, the inadequate and the timid are usually not reached by traditional provisions like youth clubs, community centres or social amenities for the handicapped and the old unless these reach out to them. The reverse side of the medal is stimulating local people to respond to the needs of vulnerable groups. Hence the term 'community care', which is applied particularly to old or handicapped people, to ex-psychiatric patients and ex-prisoners, applies also to others who cannot cope without special help and acceptance.

The search for new ways to meet unmet needs has brought professional workers out of their buildings and into the street, the pub or the coffee bar and the home.[2] Here they have discovered not only that they must have skills of a high order but also that to make contact with, for example, a youth gang is not enough. 'Going out to meet them on their own ground enables essential relationships to be made but also reinforces their detachment from the rest of the community.'[3] It has been found necessary to work not only with young people but also with their families and key residents in the community because 'youth service can only be built into a community that is functioning at a certain level of cohesion'.[4] Some of the new family advice centres set up by children's departments are also discovering that in order to do their job, they must respond to community problems by focusing on the family within the community and helping to initiate and support community action.[5]

Some of these families would function normally if certain environmental stresses were lessened; others are subject to internal psychological tensions as well as external pressures. For them new forms of social therapy, new satisfactory experiences with others, are needed to reverse long-standing anti-social attitudes and ostracism. This is difficult in itself and because it calls for concurrent change on the part of respectable neighbours and those in authority.

Part of the problem of dealing with such behaviour lies in the attitude of those with power – political, economic, or social – who work within the limits of their own rather rigid ideas about

1. Tavistock Publications, London, 1963.
2. See for example, Mary Morse, *The Unattached*, Penguin, 1965, and Goetschius and Tash, *Working with Unattached Youth*.
3. Avenues Unlimited, Technical Survey of the Second Project Report (mimeographed), 1967.
4. *Ibid.*
5. Aryeh Leissner, *Family Advice Services: Studies in Child Development*, Longmans, 1967.

society, which may have roots in the past and may not be by any means necessarily valid in the light of accurate contemporary analysis of the facts. . . . What goes wrong may partly originate in what organised society does to people.[1]

Previously we have tried to help or control the unconforming individually in difficult neighbourhoods but this usually fails unless community attitudes, or the attitudes of particular groups, can also be changed. This kind of community endeavour requires community workers who understand the roots of such behaviour, who can take hostility and frustration, but maintain their persistence and sense of direction. They need substantial training and very considerable group support and consultation.

What is known as the process oriented approach emphasises the values for group decision making, social cohesion and personality development of the processes of group interaction and achievement. It contrasts with so-called task-centred community work in which local people are stimulated to engage in some predetermined task like community care for old or handicapped people. In practice, the two approaches are interwoven with each other. The real point of difference is who determines the task. It must also be remembered that the amount which local people can achieve by their own efforts is limited. It is thus crucial that authorities providing services should be able and willing to cooperate with local action groups.

Some new 'grass roots' operational research projects make systematic use of sociological and psychological knowledge.[2] Others have been embarked on under the pressure of experience. Much more systematic enquiry and recording is needed if we are to learn from what seem to be promising new forms of social action.

LOCAL AGENCY, INTER-AGENCY AND COMMUNITY PLANNING

Grass roots community workers are part of the close and continuous two-way contact which is needed between various groups in the community and the statutory and voluntary organisations responsible for the satisfactory development of services. Other community workers may be professionals of various kinds with coordinating agency or inter-agency functions. The concept of local community planning implies that instead of the allocation of specific tasks to specific departments or individuals, to be pursued independently of each other, each service is considered in relation to the whole from the point of view of the all round needs and desires of a local community subject to pressures of social change.

1. *Difficult Housing Estates*, pp. 3 and 9.
2. See for example, John Spencer, *Stress and Release on an Urban Estate*, Tavistock Publications, London, 1964.

The aim is that responsibility for identifying new or changing needs, and taking decisions about how they should be met, should be shared between the participating organisations and the people they serve. This function entails not only a comprehensive approach to social needs but also inter-agency and interdisciplinary cooperation.

REGIONAL OR NATIONAL COMMUNITY PLANNING

We have already referred to the pressing need for comprehensive community planning not only locally but also regionally and nationally. In the sphere of physical planning this role is carried by town planners. The Town Planning Institute describes this role as follows:

> In this very often complex activity . . . persons from a number of disciplines are involved. Each plays a significant part but the chartered town planner is called upon to carry the central and crucial professional responsibility because his special skill is a command of the planning process as a whole. It is this which qualifies him to organise and co-ordinate all necessary planning operations as well as to design a plan and once it has been approved, to control its implementation and to review it.[1]

It is this kind of function which we also see emerging in the sphere of social planning. To describe what we mean we cannot do better than quote from Dr Wilfred Burns in his 1967 Presidential Address to the Institute of Town Planning:

> I believe we are driving along a cul-de-sac if we do not try to understand the relationship between environment and people's ways of living. With an understanding of this relationship there comes a greater knowledge of other factors affecting personal, family and group life and of the complete lack of any social planning aimed at helping society in a comprehensive way. . . . We are now approaching the stage where comprehensive social planning is unavoidable if we really believe in the love of human beings. We must hope that those who work in this field professionally will become better organised as a group, and we may then see the emergence of a wholly new breed of planner concerned with social planning.[2]

1. Town Planning Institute, *Progress Report on Membership Policy*, London, 1967, p. 13. The Town Planning Institute has also set up several working parties on the relation of various disciplines engaged in the common processes of urban and regional planning. One of them is on the social and allied sciences.

2. W. Burns, Presidential Address at the General Meeting of Institute of Town Planning, October 1967 reported in the *Journal of the Town Planning Institute*, vol. 53, no. 8, September/October 1967. For a general discussion see also Clarence King, *Working with People in Community Action*, Associated Press, New York, 1965, especially chapter 11, p. 3.

The Scottish White Paper, *Social Work and the Community* says:

> It seems clear that the physical environment affects social develop-
> ment and behaviour. . . . Physical planning and change involve
> social factors which in the past have not always been taken fully
> into account. This is not surprising because . . . local authorities
> responsible for these changes . . . have no officer with general
> responsibility in that field to advise them in a general and con-
> structive way at an early stage.

One of our correspondents commented:

> The Scottish White Paper . . . envisages a situation where the
> social work department is constantly being consulted on the social
> aspects of environmental changes, so that it will be able to con-
> tribute to the planning of community change at each stage. . . .
> Community work should thus not be seen merely as a third
> approach, but as something covering all three spheres of social
> work, individual, group and community.[1]

THOSE WHO EXERCISE THESE FUNCTIONS

The community work function is exercised by a few full time professional community workers, by others as a necessary part of their
professional or administrative task and by local councillors and
innumerable other voluntary workers.

There was remarkable agreement amongst those whom we
consulted about the need to provide help for a wide range of professional and voluntary workers in the understanding of cause and effect
in social intervention. We agree with Professor Donnison that they
must normally be within the power structure and that most of them
are likely to have another primary task of professional service,
planning or administration whether in public health, education,
housing, the personal social services or environmental planning.
There is in our view an emerging need, as knowledge and social
awareness increase, for people at various levels who are expert in the
social implications of decision making and implementation. Thus we
think there is also a strong case for a certain number of well-qualified
professional community workers whose appointments would be
built into the local, regional or national power structure. We do not
minimise the difficulties of this when from time to time it may be
necessary for a community worker to help local people to express
and take action about their dissatisfactions. This is not a new
problem, and it can often be wisely handled by officials and elected

1. Communication to the Study Group from Mr Gerald Popplestone, University of Aberdeen, 1967.

representatives. None the less, as we said in chapter 1, p. 4, there should always be means of effective protest and this points to the desirability of community work not only by public authorities but also by voluntary organisations whether councils of social service, special interest organisations or self help action groups. The churches could also play an effective role here.

Community work, at whatever level, is composed of the three strands of direct work with local people, of agency and inter-agency activities, and analysis, forecasting and planning. These are often interwoven in practice. Thus in the community work function the following aspects will be present in different proportions according to the nature of the task:

1. Direct work with local people in the form of a community development service. The worker will normally make himself known in a small neighbourhood for the purpose of helping local groups to define and achieve some of the goals they want. He may work for or on behalf of groups with particular needs or have a more open-ended assignment.
2. Facilitating agency and inter-agency coordination and sustaining and promoting organised groups. This includes facilitating common discussion and action between existing organisations, statutory and voluntary, and between them and the people they seek to serve in order to bring services and the meeting of need in closer relation with each other. It entails acting as an enabler, a catalyst, an adviser or an innovator of social change, according to the needs of a given situation.
3. Community planning and policy formulation. The task here is more impersonal and abstract than in direct neighbourhood or inter-agency activities. It includes the collection and presentation of relevant social data, analysis of the effects on people and on existing organisations of economic and technical developments, and of population changes on the need for services and facilities: and drawing up proposals for social policy decisions in the light of this analysis.

The foregoing are community work functions exercised by professionals or volunteers. They are practised from within various administrative frameworks which are likely to be in varying degrees compatible with the function. For example, the agency providing a direct service to individuals needs to engage in community work in order to fulfil its responsibilities. Three interrelated activities can be distinguished. First, the mobilisation of resources – the process of obtaining the funds, personnel, facilities, authority, understanding, support and so on, necessary to maintain the service. Second, the systematic development of relationships and exchanges with other bodies who can help or hinder the attainment of the objectives of the services. Third, bringing about changes in the quality and quantity of the resources necessary to provide adequate services. People will have needs which are not met or are inadequately met by existing resources, so that it is constantly necessary to change the existing arrangements in some way or to establish new provisions.

4

Employment and Career Prospects

EXISTING JOBS

This chapter examines some of the facts about existing community work posts and provides information on salary scales and career prospects. It also illustrates from a limited range of enquiries the qualifications and tasks of those at present employed in community work.

Unfortunately time and resources did not allow the Study Group to undertake a full survey of the employment field. This would be a valuable task but a difficult one because of the constantly changing situation and the lack of agreement about jobs which can be designated as community work. The variety of employments is considerable and jobs with similar content are often named differently. However this confusion about the nature of the job and the somewhat chaotic multiplicity of designations is not unique to community work.

Eileen Younghusband in her two Carnegie Trust reports on the Employment and Training of Social Workers[1] drew attention to the chaos and confusions which existed in the social work field in 1946 and 1950. T. S. Simey[2] presented a similar picture in relation to salaries and conditions of work. It was left to the Working Party on Social Workers in the Local Authority Health and Welfare Services,[3] to suggest ways of bringing some coherence to the training (or lack of it), grades of social workers and the range of their responsibilities in the local authority health and welfare services through the provision of training, employment and a career structure. The Seebohm Committee on the *Local Authority and Allied Personal Social Services*[4] is primarily required to make recommendations for the reorganisation of the relevant services but this includes the training and employment of a wide range of social workers. There are parallels in the history of many other types of employment, in local government, in education, in the youth service, where administrative reports and directives have defined more clearly the duties,

1. E. L. Younghusband, *The Employment and Training of Social Workers*, Carnegie United Kingdom Trust, 1947; and *Social Work in Britain*, Carnegie United Kingdom Trust, 1951.
2. T. S. Simey, *Salaries and Conditions of Work of Social Workers*, National Council of Social Service, London, 1947.
3. H.M.S.O., 1959 (The Younghusband Report).
4. H.M.S.O., 1968.

qualifications and salary structures for different categories of workers. Training courses leading to recognised qualifications have reinforced the trend towards a clearer definition of functions. In many cases training has led to the establishment of professional or quasi-professional grades. It is desirable that something of this same kind should happen in community work.

EMPLOYMENT PATTERNS IN FULL TIME COMMUNITY WORK

We do not know the total number of posts, their designations, nor the conditions of employment. We know relatively little about the number of new posts available, or the details of job descriptions or job analysis which might identify the scale, range and variety of functions which determine administrative and financial accountability, and which might show the opportunities for recruitment and promotion. It is hoped that an enquiry may be undertaken over the whole field.

In the meantime, some limited facts are set out below and in appendix C from information supplied to the Study Group by the National Council of Social Service and others. This information is purely illustrative and a fuller survey would certainly show a far larger number of posts, particularly in the statutory sector. Statutory employment is divided between various departments of local and other authorities, and since powers are permissive, there is no form of central registration. Thus, counting of numbers is not easy. In the voluntary sector the multiplicity of organisations also makes counting difficult. The majority of their posts are grant aided from statutory funds, thus a sharp separation between voluntary and statutory employment may not be very meaningful. In the lists of posts given in appendix C more information was available from voluntary organisations.

Face-to-face or grass roots workers (from National Council of Social Service and other data, July 1967):
1. Two hundred and fifty full time wardens in community centres known to the National Federation of Community Associations. Some centres employ assistants.
2. Thirty-two wardens of settlements. Most settlements employ several assistant staff.
3. An estimate of twenty unattached neighbourhood workers employed in experimental schemes, e.g. the North Kensington Family Study; in housing estates, e.g. the Association of London Housing Estates; in new towns, e.g. Runcorn; in community councils, e.g. Liverpool.
4. Workers with community volunteer movements and work camps; numbers not known.

Inter-agency coordination level workers (from National Council of Social Service and other data, July 1967):
1. Ninety-five full time secretaries of local councils of social service.
2. Twenty-three full time secretaries of area councils of social service.
3. Forty-two full time secretaries of rural community councils. (There is some overlap with area C.S.S.)
4. Thirty-eight full time officers of voluntary liaison committees under the National Committee for Commonwealth Immigrants.
5. Area and county secretaries in a number of national voluntary organisations, e.g. the Y.M.C.A., Y.W.C.A. or various other women's organisations, working men's clubs, etc.
6. Men and women working in the churches who play various community roles.
7. Some coordinating posts within the education, health, housing, welfare and children's departments of local authorities.
8. Social development officers in new towns.

National and regional level workers with a community work element in their roles:
1. Headquarters staff of national voluntary organisations concerned with community work, e.g. the National Council of Social Service.
2. Social scientists employed by county and other planning authorities.
3. Administrative officers at national, regional, or county level with responsibilities for community planning.
4. Social development officers with planning responsibilities in new towns (seventeen chief officers).
5. Senior research and teaching posts primarily concerned with community life and/or activities in universities and colleges of further education.

Various workers for whom community functions are subsidiary:
1. Social caseworkers engaged in services of 'community care' for the elderly, children, the handicapped, the mentally or physically ill, delinquents and ex-prisoners.
2. Adult education workers concerned with informal groups and project activities.
3. Public relations officers in local authorities.
4. Architects and town planners concerned with urban development.
5. Medical officers of health in relation to social medicine.
6. Children's officers.
7. Welfare officers.
8. Directors of education and further education officers of local authorities, head teachers.

Community Work and Social Change

9. Youth leaders and youth officers.
10. Some inspectors in central government departments.
11. Ministers of religion.

An important group includes the leaders, mostly unpaid, who are the elected representatives of local authorities and other 'community' groups, e.g. in trade unions, political organisations, religious or voluntary bodies.

The experimental course on community work organised by the National Council of Social Service from July 1966 to January 1967 included a number of participants from fields other than full time community work, e.g. housing welfare, probation and after-care, welfare services, the youth services. It was surprising to what extent discussion and job evaluation revealed a direct community content in the work of these social caseworkers and youth organisers and how relevant to their jobs they felt were the studies of community structure and community organisation, as did their employing agencies.[1]

SALARY SCALES, QUALIFICATIONS AND RECRUITMENT OF EXISTING WORKERS

In considering the extent to which community work is likely to attract candidates for training at different levels, the existing career structure is clearly important. The few available facts are given in appendix C as some indication of what now prevails. Most of the information collected came from voluntary organisations, which explains the wide differences in salaries for similar posts. The larger voluntary organisations are attempting to fix scales and to relate these to national scales in the public services: most organisations contribute towards a pension fund. Appendix C sets out some facts which illustrate the present range of recruitment, qualifications and salaries for community work posts, while the examples of advertisements for new posts also illustrate the community work element in other appointments.

JOB SPECIFICATIONS

To clarify the content and nature of jobs in community work the Study Group first undertook a general review of community work jobs and followed this by a pilot survey of eighteen community workers selected from a number of different employments. In addition, some employing agencies supplied statements setting out the duties of their workers, and the Study Group collected further

1. R. A. B. Leaper, *Community Work*, National Council of Social Service, London, 1968.

40

information as a result of advertisements for new posts in community work (see appendix C). The picture thus presented, like the data on employment, is incomplete but nevertheless illustrates the kind of posts and the nature of the work carried out by those who can reasonably be designated as full time community workers at the present time. The information was collected in 1967.

A PILOT SURVEY OF FULL TIME COMMUNITY WORKERS

Initially enquiries were undertaken by questionnaires and interviews embracing a wide range of people in different posts whose title suggested that they might be designated full time community workers. But although all were using community work methods, on enquiry many proved to have another primary function as administrators, teachers, youth officers or caseworkers. Community work was secondary to this primary role. The Study Group then invited the following organisations to suggest names of full time community workers who might be interviewed in order to discover what were their functions, skills, training and objectives:

1. The Association of Neighbourhood Workers.
2. The National Federation of Community Associations (community centre wardens).
3. The Educational Centres Association (centre wardens).
4. New Town Development Corporations (social development officers).
5. The British Association of Residential Settlements (settlement wardens).
6. The National Council of Social Service (secretaries of rural community councils).
7. The National Council of Social Service (secretaries of councils of social service).

Of the eighteen workers finally interviewed, just under half were working for statutory bodies, the remainder for voluntary organisations. Answers to four main groups of questions were obtained from standard interviews with each of them, namely:

1. What kind of work is being done?
2. What methods and skills are required to do it?
3. What are the objectives?
4. How could they be assessed?

What kind of work is being done?
Four main functions were common to all the workers, though the emphasis and the proportion of time devoted to them varied widely.

41

1. Fact finding, both by formal and informal methods. Sometimes social surveys and systematic gathering of data was attempted and related to local knowledge gained by experience.
2. Fostering of local initiative to help local groups at the grass roots or formal organisation levels to define, articulate and work towards the attainment of their interests and wants.
3. Administration of the community work agency including many office duties such as report and letter writing, finance, staff organisation and committee work. It also included creating and maintaining relations with a number of other organisations, voluntary and statutory.
4. The direct services to the community varied with the level and purposes of the agency, but often included informal and formal adult education and the provision of information. The work was often described as a communication link between the wider society and a local community, or between organisations and people. Some posts had a consultancy role, others a training role. Some workers initiated new services or promoted and sustained new groups.

What methods and skills are required?
The two skills most commonly mentioned were an ability to gather and analyse information quickly and accurately, and to establish and maintain good human relations with many different individuals, groups and organisations. There was need here both for leadership skills and for the use of group work methods. Good administration and the promotion of cooperation between many organisations, individuals and groups were recognised as essential to effective action. Committee work took up much of the time of those we interviewed and the various roles related to work with committees clearly demanded considerable skills. Public relations, supervising assistant staff, working with volunteers, and training were all discussed. Ability to communicate easily in speech and in writing, with individuals and in committee was recognised as a tool in promoting and sustaining helpful relationships.

What are the objectives?
Fundamental to all the discussions, and stated explicitly in many cases, was the endeavour to foster voluntary participation and effort in the initiation, administration and management of social services in particular and social affairs in general. All the community workers interviewed were concerned to encourage individuals and groups to accept a measure of social responsibility and were prepared to give practical support to voluntary organisations and informal groups. It was assumed by these community workers that only by participation and involvement in the affairs of the community can individuals

obtain fuller satisfaction and a greater measure of personal development in their lives. It was also thought that power and control should
not be concentrated either in the hands of political party organisations[1] or in large bureaucratic structures.

What is the effectiveness of community work?
In asking questions on the assessment of the work no clear criteria
for measurement emerged. Most workers were too busy to do more
than consider how far the demand for their services was increasing
or declining. But some thought that evidence of greater cooperation
amongst many organisations and the ability of individuals and
associations in the community to accept new ideas and approaches
were important evidence of success. The use of reporting as a tool
in evaluation was recognised, but was not used in the systematic
ways proposed in the account of the Bristol Project[2] or as has been
proposed by Dr Hendriks for use in the Netherlands.[3]

Other evidence, on the content of the job and some of the methods
employed came from participants in the community work course
run by the National Council of Social Service referred to on p. 40.
Each kept a detailed diary for a typical week. Some impressions
which emerged of the patterns of work were the following:

> The first impression from the diaries is that the lives of these
> community workers consisted largely of short and rapid contacts
> with a wide variety of people. Sometimes they contact the clients
> of the organisation, sometimes other collaborating agencies or
> public authorities, and many times colleagues whom the workers
> wish to consult. But the general picture is of over-worked, rather
> harried people, moving from one job to another, constantly on the
> telephone, writing memoranda, or keeping urgent appointments.
> The second general impression is of the very highly structured
> society within which the workers operate. . . . The network of
> contacts and influences was complex and at times confusing . . .
> the essential skills and techniques of their job were to know these
> networks and how to use them. . . . Hence, the large amount of
> time spent on letters, memoranda, phone calls and personal
> meetings. . . . A minority are in contact with individuals who were
> in need of help . . . concerned with after-care, with housing, with
> social work in a welfare department. Even these workers spent a
> lot of time on a whole host of other jobs at one remove from the
> client or his family. . . . Everybody attended committee meetings

1. For a discussion of this see *Management of Local Government*, vol. 1,
especially para. 32.
2. J. Spencer, *Stress and Release on an Urban Estate*.
3. G. Hendriks, *Social Planning and Community Development*, the Netherlands
Ministry of Culture, Recreation and Social Welfare, 1964.

or association meetings. . . . Many workers had to spend quite a lot of their time on minutes, reports and account keeping.[1]

CAREER PROSPECTS

The new posts described in appendix C are a small selection from a number of appointments in current advertisements. It is clear that there is an expanding field for the employment of full time community workers but, as yet, no estimates of future trends. We do not know the channels for recruitment, the prospects for promotion nor the relative emphasis employers are likely to place on experience compared with training. These are questions that need to be clarified if community work training is to compete with established careers attracting well motivated and capable people. Can a new entrant expect to start with neighbourhood and grass roots work and then move up to the more administrative tasks of inter-agency work?

Some claim that different personal qualities as well as some differences in training are needed between these types of work, others emphasise the common element between neighbourhood and inter-agency work and consider that with additional training, plus experience, transfer to community planning is likely for some workers. it would be unfortunate if movement up an administrative ladder were to become the only yardstick of success when here, as in other professions, seniority and a recognised status are greatly needed at the grass roots level. It is also important that there should be career opportunities which cross departmental frontiers. The history of the youth service is an unhappy illustration of difficulties of transfer; casework has had similar problems of a fragmented employment structure.

FORECASTS OF FUTURE DEMANDS

The many government enquiries referred to in chapter 2 could, if implemented, create overwhelming demands for community workers in relation to training resources. The report on *The Needs of New Communities* suggests in chapter 5 the need to appoint in overspill areas, new housing estates and new towns, arrivals officers and social relations officers with ancillary staff. These officers, it is suggested, are needed in expansion schemes where the populations are in the order of ten thousand and above.

Nineteen expansion schemes with increased populations of over ten thousand have been agreed under the Town Development Act 1952, and ten more with population increases just below ten thousand. These figures do not include housing estates, the Scottish figures, nor those for new towns. The Seebohm Committee had not reported

1. R. A. B. Leaper, 'The Tasks of Community Workers', mimeographed report on N.C.S.S. training course, October 1966, p. 5.

when the present report was written. In evidence to it the Joint University Council for Social and Public Administration suggested that in each county and county borough there should be a community work officer for duties of coordination, as one of a team of senior social workers. Each district office should include a neighbourhood community worker. In 1967 there were fifty-nine county councils and eighty-two county boroughs in England and Wales, and thirty-two London boroughs, so, assuming an average of three districts in each area, these recommendations would create a need for 519 neighbourhood workers and 173 senior community workers. If the preventive and supportive work envisaged in the Children and Young Persons Act, 1963, in the schemes for community care in the health and welfare services, in prison after-care, or in work in deprived neighbourhoods, are to become realities, the recommendations of the J.U.C. seem eminently sensible. The training and staffing implications are clear. We already have some evidence from Scotland where posts in community work are clearly foreshadowed in the White Paper on *Social Work and the Community*[1] and are implicit in the Social Work (Scotland) Act, 1968.

Such forecasts are conjectures at this stage, but are nevertheless important in drawing attention to the need to establish, as we suggest in chapter 12, a council which in addition to other training duties would have the responsibility to keep under review employment and training needs, and to help in the planning of a coherent career structure in what is now a fragmented field of work.

LEGAL POWERS AND EMPLOYING AGENCIES

The facts set out in the previous pages say little about who are the employing bodies and nothing about the legal enactments which give statutory authorities the powers to employ community workers, or powers to grant aid to voluntary organisations for these purposes. A complex and difficult question in urgent need of clarification is administrative responsibility for community work. At present there are various clauses under different Acts of Parliament, which give permissive powers for the employment of community workers or for grant aid to voluntary organisations for this purpose. A full table of these many Acts is set out as appendix C in the Report on *The Needs of New Communities* (pp. 98–102). They include:

1. The Education Act 1944, Section 41.
2. The Physical Training and Recreation Act 1937, Section 4.
3. The Housing Act 1957, Section 93.
4. The Local Government Act 1948, Section 132.
5. The Local Government (Financial Provisions) Act 1963, Section 6.

1. H.M.S.O., 1967.

Other powers are conferred by the National Assistance Act 1948 and the National Health Service Act 1946, for particular groups. The responsible authority is usually the county and county borough council.

Because the legislation is divided, employment and finance are also divided. There is considerable confusion at central government level as to which Ministry, Education and Science, Housing and Local Government, Health, or Home Office, is primarily interested in the development and sponsorship of community work. All have some interest but this is inevitably a departmental interest. At local government level the same confusion exists between the education, housing, planning, health, welfare and children's departments. The probation and after-care service also has specific community tasks.

In some cases the Clerk has taken direct responsibility. There are, in addition, the statutory bodies set up under regional planning legislation or for the administration of new towns. Voluntary organisations themselves represent a complexity of different initiatives, with differing conceptions of community work, different sources of finance and differing conditions of employment. The National Council of Social Service has provided one major element of coordination in the voluntary field, as yet largely lacking in the statutory services.

Three main issues arise from the diversity of employing agencies. The first is that an activity which is not the primary responsibility of one Ministry may be allowed to drift. The keen interest in community work by the then Ministry of Education at the end of the 1939–45 war, was not followed up, and a similar situation developed under the then Ministry of Town and Country Planning. What happens at central government level is reflected in local government. Because legislation is permissive, if there is no strong initiative from any of the major departments many local authorities do little or nothing to promote the employment of community workers. The new towns by way of contrast, under active leadership from the centre, have created a number of posts (seventeen social development officers and thirty-four assistants with extensive staff) and there is a clear statement of duties and objectives published by the Ministry of Housing and Local Government[1] (for an example see appendix C).

The second issue, and by far the most difficult, is that community work by its very nature is not concerned with a single department nor a single function. At grass roots level it seeks to be a communication link between a number of groups and organisations. Inter-agency and planning work are by definition coordinating activities.

1. Ministry of Housing and Local Government *Handbook*, issued to the New Town Development Corporations, 1965, appendix C.

To say this does not necessarily mean that community work should not start from a firm administrative base. As is pointed out in various contexts in this report, the reality of community work is that it is likely to be concerned with specific activities by particular groups: the provision of recreational facilities in a new housing estate, the development of opportunities for handicapped persons to enjoy social contacts, or the coordination of social with economic aspects of planning in a region. The work starts from a base but spreads out across normal departmental frontiers. Because it involves people and their relationships with administration, community work cannot easily confine itself to a single departmental approach. It works up and down between the people and the many organisations that serve them and at the organisational level between many departments and voluntary bodies. This network aspect is brought out in the account of community workers' tasks in chapter 3.

It is important that the reality of this position should be recognised and that Ministries and local government departments should create posts which allow for flexibility of approach in multiple relationships with people and in the coordinating activities between administrative agencies.

The third issue arising from the divisions of legislation and employment relates to the problem that individual workers with essentially common professional tasks are given different designations, salaries and promotion opportunities according to the department or voluntary organisation which happens to employ them. The survey of community workers' activities on pp. 41–2 above showed the degree to which the content of the job, the skills and the methods of work were similar despite the variety of employing agencies. This suggests that the several Ministries, local government associations, the major voluntary organisations, the professional organisations and the educational bodies must agree on some common standards for community work. Such agreement could provide a basis for recognising qualifications, for establishing some comparable salary scales and for creating a career structure which allows for mobility based on professional competence. At present community workers may belong to various professional associations, but there is fragmentation here as elsewhere. It is to be hoped that current developments in the Standing Conference of Organisations of Social Workers and elsewhere will help to clarify the situation.

Chapters 2 and 12 touch on the number of government and other committees which are at present, among other matters, considering questions which relate to community work. It would be a tragedy if these many separate reports were to lead to an even greater fragmentation in the training and employment of community workers.

5

Provision for Study of Community Work in Courses in Universities and other Educational Institutions

HOW THE INFORMATION WAS OBTAINED

In an attempt to obtain a picture of provision for study of community work, a questionnaire[1] was submitted in 1967 to: every university social studies (or similarly named) department in membership of the Joint University Council for Social and Public Administration; London University Institute of Education and Queen Elizabeth College (London); the Adult Education Department of the Faculty of Education (Manchester); adult education and extra-mural departments of all universities; colleges of further education with courses for the certificate in social work or the letter of recognition in child care; the National College for the Training of Youth Leaders; two Scottish colleges of education (Jordanhill and Moray House); Westhill College of Education (course for community centre wardens). An enquiry was also made to some colleges of education in England and Wales with a third-year option in youth leadership, and to residential adult education colleges.

The questionnaire asked: 'Do you have any provision within your teaching and research programme for courses in community development, community organisation, community work?'

'Community work' was said to be dealt with more frequently than the other two: but this was largely due to (a) the apparent ambiguity of the term to many respondents, and (b) the large number of courses primarily designed for potential workers in specified fields like child care, social work in health and welfare departments or youth work, where any consideration of the community implications of the worker's professional task was described as 'community work'.

Several members of the Study Group engaged in education and training related to community work supplemented the information obtained by correspondence.

Courses in sociology departments which examine theoretically such questions as concepts of community, social structure, or methods of social investigation were not included. It is, however, clear from other chapters that we consider such studies important for community workers. It seems likely, too, that some sociology graduates become community workers, but we have scant information on this point. We are also aware of the wide range of relevant

1. This questionnaire was sent out by Mr R. A. B. Leaper in January 1967.

studies in industrial sociology, economics, management studies, the social aspects of town planning and regional development, local government and administration.

The information which follows is based upon replies received from universities and colleges to whom the questionnaire was sent. Some who may have courses to which reference should have been made did not respond, while the amount of information given by those who did is uneven. Thus it is not claimed that the material in this chapter gives a comprehensive account of the situation in 1967.

UNIVERSITY INTERNAL SOCIAL STUDIES AND OTHER DEPARTMENTS

Out of thirty-eight university departments approached seventeen departments which replied reported some relevant provision in their teaching and research programmes. Of these, eleven said that they had lecture courses in community development, twelve in community organisation, and nine in community work. That is to say, several have more than one course. Five courses consisted only of occasional lectures from visiting lecturers and two of short optional extra courses. Nine universities provided lecture courses in their first degree syllabus; five in courses given in diploma syllabuses, and nine in the applied social studies course leading to a professional casework qualification. The length and type varied greatly. In one university, courses were run on a mixed lecture and tutorial basis, 'each student having about 220 hours'. The remainder varied between twenty-five and eight lecture periods. Community fieldwork was compulsory for those taking the community work sequence in seven departments and in six others it was optional. The length was unspecified in six cases and in the remainder (where specified) varied between a six to eight week block, a ten to twelve week concurrent placement during term time, and (in one case) a total length of 'about 150 hours'.

First (i.e. pre-professional) degree or diploma courses included community work as an integral part of an introductory social work course. In eleven such cases students were expected to cover their community work knowledge as part of a general examination paper in social work, while in two others it was a separate paper.

Nine of the one-year post-graduate applied social studies courses for professional casework training included the community implications of a caseworker's job in their general examinations.

Four universities reported some research in community organisation; two of them were making long-term surveys of new towns and their social provisions; one undertook research on training for community work, one made regular provision for dissertations for higher degrees to include community work subjects, while in three other cases there were minor short-term projects in progress. The full time courses in community development are described in more detail below.

Full time courses in community development, primarily for work overseas

The University of Manchester (Department of Adult Education) one-year diploma of advanced studies in community development includes principles and methods of community development, the social framework, communication techniques, community organisation, the organisation and techniques of adult literacy teaching and techniques of simple surveys and fact finding. There is also practical work in fact finding and surveys during the course. Some of the lecture courses are also taken by students reading for the diploma in adult education and the diploma in youth work.

The University of Edinburgh (Department of Adult Education) one-year post-graduate diploma in community development and youth studies includes substantially the same subjects, i.e. theory and practice of community development, techniques of communication, economic problems of developing countries, comparative social organisation, youth studies and group work theory, adult education in developing countries, adult literacy work, agricultural extension, health education, and services for youth. Students have an opportunity to study efforts to improve conditions in both urban and rural areas.

At University College, Swansea, the two-year diploma in social development and social administration includes the development of social services in Britain, economics of developing countries, community development, the sociology of developing societies, government and administration, principles and methods of social work. This allows for specialisation in community work throughout the second year; about half the first-year lectures, seminars and the concurrent fieldwork are concerned with group and community work. Those who take the second-year option have, as well as their lectures, a six-week block placement in community development and a two to three week block placement in community organisation. Students have eighteen weeks fieldwork during the course, and some concurrent and some short block placements in community agencies.

The Manchester course is intended as a training for community development either in this country or overseas. The Edinburgh course is primarily intended for overseas students, though British students may be admitted. The Swansea course is generally taken by those who intend to work in rapidly developing countries but some British students for the degree or diploma in social administration also take this community work option. Similarly, the courses at the London School of Economics form part of a university training in social administration: in the M.Sc. in social administration and social work studies there is now an optional paper in community development.

The University of London Institute of Education provides a three months in-service training course for senior officers of government departments and voluntary agencies from both 'developing' and 'developed' countries.[1]

Queen Elizabeth College (University of London) has a one-year post-graduate diploma in home economics related to community development for experienced men and women from overseas. It includes courses on the social structure of contemporary society, methods and techniques in adult education and methods of communication. There is no practical work.

UNIVERSITY EXTRA-MURAL DEPARTMENTS

Nine extra-mural departments out of twenty-four approached made some form of provision. In five cases this was confined to occasional lectures or to short courses of either less than ten consecutive lectures or a residential weekend. Four had sessional lecture courses, and one a course which was part of a degree requirement. The majority of the courses consisted of about twenty lectures with related private reading (two with a total length of twenty to twenty-four hours). Only one of the courses included fieldwork, lasting for two to three weeks. Only one extra-mural department was undertaking a research project – a new town study, financed from the funds of the department. Several others mentioned brief local community surveys. Eight such departments run two-year child care courses. Only one of these mentioned a lecture course (with related fieldwork) in community development. One adult education department, which is starting a course for experienced child care officers in 1968, intends to include an initial placement in a community work agency together with three or four lectures on community work as a social work method.

COLLEGES OF FURTHER EDUCATION

1. Courses for the certificate in social work

Questionnaires were sent to twenty-one colleges of further education providing these courses, of which sixteen replied. Ten stated that they made no provision for community work. Three provided only occasional lectures or series of lectures giving information about

1. For a detailed account of methods used in this course see two books by T. R. Batten, *Training for Community Development*, Oxford University Press, 1962, and *The Non-Directive Approach*, Oxford University Press, 1967.

community development or community organisation principles and methods. Three made more substantial provision; for example, one provided twelve weekly lecture/discussions with a social worker in a community development project. Students also went on visits of observation to councils of social service. Another course sent students on a four-month placement with a community association, preparing them by a day's teaching a week on group dynamics and general problems of group work. A third course included lectures on community development and housing in its programme, and eight lectures on 'work with groups' together with eight days' observation with a community association. The general position seems fairly summarised by two typical explanatory comments: (*a*) 'Naturally one of the threads running through the course is that of "community care" . . . one of the objectives of the course is to help students to be more aware of, and able to use, the community network in a conscious way in their role as local government social workers'; (*b*) 'In summary, the aim of our course is to train social workers to work in the community setting rather than to provide students with any formal training as community workers as such.'

2. Child care courses

Questionnaires were sent to fourteen colleges providing recognised courses, of which twelve replied. Nine stated that they made no provision for community work. Two provided occasional lectures on community development or community organisation. In one college prolonged visits of observation in the first term included settlements. This course also had ten hours of lectures and discussions on community work including lectures by a worker in an urban community development project. Occasionally students on this course have a three-week placement with this worker.

SCOTTISH COLLEGES OF EDUCATION: MORAY HOUSE AND JORDANHILL

It should be remembered that the role of colleges of education in Scotland is somewhat different from that of their opposite numbers in England and Wales. With the support and encouragement of the Scottish Standing Advisory Committee for Youth and Community Service, Moray House (Edinburgh) and Jordanhill (Glasgow) provide two-year courses leading to a diploma in youth and community service. These courses are mainly concerned with the youth service but they are based on the assumption that youth work should be seen in the context of the local community. Thus they include group work in the community and the principles and practice of community development and organisation. Fieldwork forms an integral part of the courses at both colleges. The first-year syllabus at Moray House is largely taken in common with students on two-year courses for the certificate in social work and the letter of recognition in child care. At this college an average of twenty students a year have successfully completed the diploma in youth and community service courses in each of the last four years, and of these about a third are engaged in specifically designated 'community work'.

TRAINING FOR COMMUNITY CENTRE WARDENS

Westhill College of Education, Birmingham, provides a two-year course sponsored by the Department of Education and Science for community centre wardens. Grant aid is only available for five students a year, though this is the only substantial vocational course in community work as such in England and Wales. The students train alongside teachers and youth and church workers. The syllabus includes community organisation, social group work, casework and management skills. The minimum age for admission is twenty-five years. Equal time is given to theory and practice, integrated through tutorial sessions. Students spend about half the first year in full time work at a community centre under the supervision of a professional warden. They also have three vacation periods of three to four weeks in community centres; with a community association without a professional warden; and with a council of social service. Visits of observation are paid to other community centres, to new towns and to other social work institutions. Successful students receive the University of Birmingham Institute of Education certificate for community centre wardens.

In 1966 the Joint National Council for Youth Leaders and Community Centre Wardens decided that those employed as full time community centre wardens should have a professional qualification if their salaries were to be grant-aided by local education authorities. In addition to those already qualified on the Westhill course, those with five or more years satisfactory experience were recognised as qualified by experience. Qualifying courses for other wardens who are not recognised as qualified by either of the above mentioned means are being organised by the Department of Education and Science. The first was a seven-week residential course run in 1967 at Shoreditch College of Education, Surrey. It was organised under the auspices of the Inner London Education Authority and taken by thirty practising community centre wardens. The syllabus included lectures, discussion, and required reading on group work, community organisation, social psychology, management skills and craftwork, and also a community survey which formed part of the material for the final assessment.

TRAINING FOR YOUTH WORK

Apart from the third-year options taken at some colleges of education, there are post-graduate courses for youth workers at Manchester University, and University College, Swansea, and for other candidates in the two-year course at Westhill College, but the majority of youth work students take the one-year course at the National College for the Training of Youth Leaders at Leicester. The courses at Swansea and Leicester are intended to qualify candidates (at different educational levels) for the youth service. The Manchester course combines training for different types of work with young people, and students are able to take the community development option in the Adult Education Department. In all these courses there is some consideration of community structure and interaction, and the relation of youth work to other activities in the community.

COLLEGES OF EDUCATION IN ENGLAND AND WALES

Thirty colleges of education in England and Wales offer a youth leadership option in their three-year training courses. Only ten options have existed long enough to provide useful information. Full information, including the syllabus of theoretical and practical training, was obtained from seven of these colleges. While none would claim that it is training for community work, it is clear that much of the content is relevant to this. One course aims at developing students' ability to assess the effect and nature of the environment in which they are working with young people, another includes principles and methods of social investigation, including techniques of investigation, a group research project, social experiment, and investigations in evaluation.

There is little evidence that students who have taken these options are going into full time youth work. This is unlikely in view of the career structure of the teaching profession, yet teachers with this option are likely to work with the local community in a variety of ways. A number of openings today include not only the posts of teacher/warden, teacher/youth leader, and similar appointments, but also posts involving community work within the school, in its relationships with the local community in general and in particular with the social services.

RESIDENTIAL ADULT EDUCATION COLLEGES

The eight colleges to which questionnaires were sent aim at general education rather than vocational training. Five provided some teaching about communities. None had any research projects.

NUMBERS COMPLETING UNIVERSITY COURSES WHICH INCLUDE
COMMUNITY WORK
(Information supplied by universities, 1967)

| University | Numbers completing courses* | | | | Numbers on current courses* 1966/67 |
	1964	1965	1966	Total	
BIRMINGHAM					
Dip. in Soc. Work	32	32	32	96	32
B.Soc.Sc. (Soc. Study)	32	29	29	90	36
DUBLIN (*National Univ.*)					
B.Soc.Sc.	13	16	—	29	93
EDINBURGH					
Cert. in Child Care, Medical Social Work, and Psychiatric Social Work	—	—	18	18	24
Post-graduate Dip. in community development	—	—	6	6	10
LONDON					
(*a*) *Inst. of Ed.*					
Community devel. course	16	13	13	42	13
(*b*) *L.S.E.*					
1 yr. graduate Dip. in Soc. Admin.	5	8	6	19	—
Two yr. non-grad. Dip. in Soc. Admin.	33	9	10	52	10+
Post-grad.: M.Sc. Econ.	—	—	3	3	—
MANCHESTER					
Dip. in community devel.	12	16	17	45	20
NEWCASTLE					
B.A. (social studies)	20	25	25	70	35
NOTTINGHAM					
B.A. (Soc. Admin.)	25	33	32	90	33
Dip. in Applied Soc. Studies	9	18	13	40	20
SWANSEA					
Dip. in Soc. Admin.	17	16	22	55	20
Dip. in Soc. Policy	20	19	21	60	22
Dip. in Soc. Development	16	17	19	52	39 (19 1st yr. 20 2nd yr.)
B.Sc.(Econ.)	—	—	—	—	3

* These figures do not include those taking optional courses.

Notes.

1. The diploma courses in social policy and in social development at Swansea; in social administration at L.S.E. (with community development); and the diploma courses in community development at Manchester and Edinburgh are all largely for overseas students.
2. In the years 1964/6 it is estimated that about twenty-four of those completing the courses in these tables entered community work in Britain, and another four in Ireland (from University College, Dublin).
3. The youth courses at Manchester and Swansea are in the Adult Education and Education Departments.

PROVISION FOR STUDY OF COMMUNITY WORK IN UNIVERSITY AND OTHER COURSES; U.K.*

(Based on information supplied by universities and colleges, 1967)

	Only occasional lectures/ short courses	'Sustained' provisions	In 1st degree courses	In dip. and cert. courses	In applied social studies courses	Other sessional courses	Fieldwork compulsory	Fieldwork optional	Separate exam. in subject	Qualification in 'community' mentioned	Research projects	Outside finance for research
University social study and other departments (17/38)	7	10	9	4	8	1	7	6	3	4	6	5
University extra-mural departments (9/24)	5	4	1	–	–	3	–	4	–	–	1	–
Colleges of further education Cert. in soc. work courses (6/21)	3	3	–	1	–	–	2	4	–	–	–	–
Child care courses (3/14)	2	1	–	–	–	–	–	–	3	–	–	–
Residential adult education colleges (5/8)	5	–	–	–	–	–	–	2	–	–	–	–
The National College for the Training of Youth Leaders (1/1)	–	1	–	1	–	–	1	–	–	–	–	–
Scottish colleges of education (2/2)	–	2	–	–	–	2	2	–	2	2	–	–
Westhill College of Education (course for community centre wardens)	–	1	–	1	–	–	1	–	1	1	–	–

* And University College, Dublin, which is affiliated to the J.U.C.

The above table is based upon provisions stated to be made as follows:

University social study and other departments. Birmingham, Bath, U.C. Dublin, Edinburgh (social study and adult education departments), Kent at Canterbury, Keele, Leicester, London (L.S.E., Inst. of Ed., and Q. Elizabeth), Manchester (adult ed.), Newcastle, Nottingham, Sussex, Swansea and York.

University extra-mural departments. Birmingham, Bristol, Cambridge, Glasgow, Keele, Leicester, Liverpool, Nottingham, Southampton, Swansea.

Cert. in social work courses. Birmingham College of Commerce, Barking College of Technology, Bristol College of Commerce, Ipswich Civic College, Sheffield College of Technology, Manchester College of Commerce.

Child care courses. Cardiff College of Commerce, North-Western Polytechnic, Plymouth College of Technology.

Residential Adult Education Colleges. Co-operative College; Catholic Workers' College; Coleg Harlech; Ruskin College, Oxford; Newbattle Abbey College, Dalkeith; Hillcroft College, Surbiton; Fircroft College, Birmingham.

The National College for the Training of Youth Leaders.

Scottish Colleges of Education. Moray House (Edinburgh) and Jordanhill (Glasgow).

Westhill College of Education (course for community centre wardens).

OTHER PROVISIONS IN BRITAIN

There are many short-term in-service or short refresher courses provided by local education authorities in colleges of further education and elsewhere, university extra-mural departments, adult education bodies, councils of social service, etc., for community centre wardens, adult education workers, councils of social service personnel and also voluntary workers.

The first course specifically for 'community workers' of all kinds was run in 1966–7, under the auspices of the National Council of Social Service aided by the Gulbenkian Foundation. It lasted for seven months and consisted of an initial and a final residential period of a fortnight and a week, a programme of reading and a community survey project, together with job analyses. The fieldwork included eight visits to another agency. Part-time consultants gave tutorial help. The participants included community centre wardens, council of social service personnel, wardens of settlements and social workers in probation and prison after-care, health and welfare and housing departments of local authorities, each of whom considered the implications of community care for his job (see chapter 4, p. 40).

A six months' sandwich course consisting of three separate weeks of theoretical studies, with projects in the intervening periods back at work, was started by the National Institute for Social Work Training in 1968 for participants engaged in community work. It has also set up a five-year project in community work in Southwark as an element in plans to establish a full time training in social work with communities within the next two years. The aim of the field project will be not only to help in the community selected, but also to evaluate the possibilities of field training, to provide teaching material, and to develop fieldwork placements.

The University of York started a community organisation project in 1967 with the dual purpose of identifying and taking action to meet social needs in York and teaching community organisation to students. Since 1966 the University of Liverpool has had a research fellow and tutor in community organisation whose work includes seminars for a group of community workers and lecturing to students at local teacher training and theological colleges.

In 1968 the Joint University Council for Social and Public Administration decided to set up a group to survey community work provisions in existing university courses, to consider problems of fieldwork and to encourage the development of these courses in universities.

The Institute of Local Government Studies (Birmingham University), which has for several years run courses for overseas senior administrators, started in 1967 a ten weeks' advanced course for senior local government officers. This staff college type of course is intended for those who are, or will shortly be, responsible for advising their authority or administering policies. The course includes sociological analysis of communities, current trends and social and cultural change. The aim is to give 'senior local government officers the opportunity to reflect on the nature of their work for communities faced with unprecedented technological and social challenges'.[1]

We have already described in chapter 2, pp. 14–15, the Treasury courses for civil servants.

SUMMARY OF THE BRITISH SITUATION IN 1967

1. Of the university diploma and degree courses described, nine had at least one lecture a week for a ten-week term on community organisation and community development, usually with short visits of observation. Four provided at least weekly lectures for a year or more, combined with vacation fieldwork of one short and one six- or eight-week placement with a community centre, community association, settlement or council of social service.[2]

2. In professional social work courses community work is almost wholly confined to lectures or discussions about the community implications of a caseworker's job or to short lecture courses with field observation of community development.

3. The university courses of training for community development are mainly for overseas students or for those intending to work in rapidly developing countries, although a few British students are now beginning to take these courses. Some already have experience in community work situations in Britain; others apply with the intention of employment in it.

4. There is professional training for community centre wardens at Westhill College of Education. In a transitional period a number of 'qualifying' courses are to be provided of which the first was at Shoreditch College of Education in 1967.

5. Professional training for some teachers and for youth leaders includes an element of community work, but it is clearly seen as an aspect of the work of a teacher or a youth leader, not as training for professional community work as such.

6. A variety of other in-service and *ad hoc* provisions exist and will no doubt be extended. At present these are sometimes a substitute for systematic training on a scale wide enough to ensure uniform standards of qualification and professional recognition.

7. As with the development of other forms of social work training, one of the main problems is that of organising satisfactory fieldwork, in which a distinction has to be made between observation and training in practice skills. At present the settings most used are councils of social service, settlements and community centres. The development of closer relationships between training institutions

1. Prospectus of advanced courses for senior local government officers, 1968, University of Birmingham, Institute of Local Government Studies.

2. Leaflets on course content and organisation, University of Edinburgh, London School of Economics, University of Manchester (Department of Adult Education), University of Nottingham, University College of Swansea.

and agencies able to offer field supervision is essential. Some experiments have been successfully tried of group exercises in community development projects both in Britain and in other countries. Sheffield Council of Social Service has recently formulated plans for a community organisation training unit in conjunction with the University, and Swansea University College has similar plans. The National Institute for Social Work Training programme and plans at the University of York have already been mentioned. In community work training a combination of concurrent theory and practice is recognised as essential and increased attention is being paid to field-work placements, supervision and assessment. This is discussed in chapter 11.

COMMUNITY WORK TRAINING IN OTHER COUNTRIES

While neither resources nor space allow a comprehensive review of community work training in other countries, some notes on the United States and the Netherlands may be useful for comparison.

The United States
Students with a bachelor's degree take a two-year post-graduate master's degree in social work with a 'concentration' in community organisation. Some twenty-five university schools of social work have now extended the second year concentration on community organisation to two full years of field practice and class work, while approximately another twenty schools offer the course in the second year. Many schools include community organisation concepts and methods, in an introductory form, in their curricula for caseworkers and group workers. A few schools are experimenting with various curricula that combine casework, group work and community organisation methods into 'training for social work', as well as with combining community organisation with research or administration.

In recent years there has been a rapid increase in the number of schools of social work offering this concentration and the proportion of students selecting it far outstrips the rate of growth of the total number of social work students. Thus from 1961 to 1965 total enrolment increased by 55 per cent but the number of those concentrating on community organisation rose by 400 per cent. In 1966 there were 789 community organisation students.

This remarkable growth partly reflects the demands of many new social programmes for staffs with organising and planning skills and the interest of young people in social reform and action at the community level, an interest stimulated by the civil rights movement, the war on poverty and the Peace Corps. In 1965 a three-year project on community organisation curriculum development was started.

It is financed by the Federal Government, administered by the Council on Social Work Education, and carried out at Brandeis University. The project is to present its recommendations and teaching materials in the autumn of 1968.[1]

There is some tendency for schools of social work to emphasise one or another aspect of community work, often in line with the experience and interests of the faculty. Thus some stress neighbourhood organisation or social action at the grass roots, others inter-organisational planning of services. But in general they introduce students to the full range of practice. Fieldwork, once limited to welfare councils, neighbourhood centres and similar organisations, is now being carried on in a wide range of settings; for example, the offices of mayors and governors, trade unions, urban renewal and housing programmes, civil rights organisations, community mental health centres, and particularly neighbourhood-oriented programmes which are part of the war on poverty. Where there is no trained social work supervisor at the field placement, the university faculty helps the student to examine his field experience and performance. Several schools are moving away from the practice of placing a student for a year in one agency and experimenting with a number of short-term, carefully chosen experiences, involving observation and actual engagement, while at the same time retaining a primary attachment to one organisation.

The considerable variation in curricula among schools has been noted. But this is always within the three divisions of (1) human behaviour and the social environment, (2) social welfare policy and services and (3) methods of social work practice (in this case, community organisation).[2] The first category includes the application to practice of findings and concepts from psychology, sociology, anthropology, political science, economics and social research method.

Experimentation is also in progress with curricula that combine community organisation with administration (i.e. agency management) or with research, or with urban and community planning. In addition there are scattered efforts to find common ground and to share in field experiences and hold joint seminars with professional schools in such closely related studies as physical planning, public health, and public administration. It is increasingly recognised that practitioners in these fields are heavily engaged in various aspects of community work.[3]

1. For further references see chapter 6, p. 69, and chapter 9, p. 116.

2. This is in line with the *Statement on Curriculum Policy*, Council on Social Work Education, New York, 1962.

3. We are indebted to Professor Robert Perlman of Brandeis University for this summary of information about the United States position. For details see: *Progress Reports*, Community Organisation Curriculum Development Project, Council on Social Work Education, New York, 1966.

The Netherlands

Social work training in the Netherlands is provided in independent 'social academies' whose graduates receive a diploma which is the recognised professional qualification for social work. Besides training in casework, various social academies also run courses for youth leaders, personnel officers, 'cultural workers', and community workers. The admission requirement is completion of secondary school education. The Rotterdam Academy has a four-year course in community organisation, of which the first two and the last are spent in theoretical studies, and the third year in practical work under supervision. Like other courses, this combines general education in social studies, including philosophy, psychology, sociology, economics, civics and government, with training in general social work, group work and community organisation. The Catholic Academy at The Hague provides a similar course.

The growing interest in training for community development and community organisation is a comparatively recent development. In 1960 Dr G. Hendriks could write: 'In the Netherlands there does not exist, as yet, any training which is directed completely to this new field of activity, although a few schools of social work have attempted to adapt their existing programmes to these requirements. At university level also the implications of training in this field have not yet been realised.'[1] Nevertheless the concern for urban renewal and the growth of new housing areas, as well as the social and economic transformation of much of the countryside by wide-scale planning, such as the Polder reclamation and the Scheldt development areas, have called for many more workers with community work qualifications.

At Nijmegen University there is a part-time two-year advanced course of in-service training in community organisation for students already holding a social academy diploma. At the universities of Gröningen and Amsterdam a course in community development is being discussed for inclusion in sociology courses. It is expected that in 1968 two new advanced two-year courses in community organisation will be established at Rotterdam and Nijmegen for social academy and university graduates.

There is a six months course in practical skills in community development for overseas voluntary workers at the Amsterdam Tropical Institute and a two-year training in community development at Cudenbroek for members of religious orders working in Africa. The Institute of Social Studies at The Hague provides a number of courses in community development mainly for students from Asia and Africa.

1. G. Hendriks, *Community Organisation*, the Netherlands Ministry of Cultural Affairs, Recreation and Social Welfare, 1964, p. 7.

Community Work and Social Change

In accordance with a decision taken at an European Consultation on Training for Community Development held in the Netherlands in 1967, an European Regional Clearing House for Community Work has now been opened at 146 Stadhourderslaan, The Hague, Holland. It will be concerned with community projects of all kinds, including training provisions, and will publish a quarterly communication and information bulletin. The Secretariat is to be provided by the Netherlands Institute of Community Development in collaboration with the Netherlands Ministry of Cultural Affairs, Recreation and Social Welfare.[1]

1. We are indebted to Dr W. A. C. Zwanniken of the Netherlands Institute of Community Development and Mr C. Eckhart of the Netherlands Ministry of Cultural Affairs, Recreation and Social Welfare for the information used in this section.

PART TWO

Functions and Aims

6

The Functions of Community Workers

INTRODUCTION[1]

Having considered the current situation, the next step is a detailed analysis of the functions and tasks of community workers. These are different from social or community processes *per se*, such as conflict, cooperation or change, which form much of the situation within which the work is done. The focus in this chapter is on the worker in action and what he does, the skills he requires and how he performs his functions. These are discussed in relation to training in chapters 10 and 11.

The activities described below, which apply to community work in all settings, are aspects of a problem-solving process. In addition there are differences in the tasks performed by community workers according to the circumstances in which they work and the factors that distinguish one type of community work from another.

Statutory and voluntary organisations which employ community workers (or have members of their staff who devote part of their time to community work) do so as a means of carrying out the organisation's purposes, for example, the promotion of voluntary services for the elderly, the development of a local mental health service, the strengthening of neighbourly relationships, or the expansion of facilities for the handicapped. The purpose of the employing organisation sets limits to the kind of community work and has a strong influence on the direction it will take.

Organisations with broad purposes select from time to time specific social problems on which to work. The character of these also shapes a community worker's activities. The very way in which an organisation defines a problem situation suggests certain kinds of activities and excludes others. One would not expect a child care officer who is promoting a family advice centre to mobilise a public protest against council members opposed to the idea. Nor would a neighbourhood worker who is assisting a tenants' association to obtain more play facilities for children undertake a three-year study of land use in the borough. The appropriateness of action by a community worker is, then, largely shaped by the kind of organisation for which he works and by the particular project or problem with which he is concerned.

Account must also be taken of the interests, needs and wishes of groups and organisations other than the one that employs the

1. This chapter is largely the work of Professor Robert Perlman of the Community Organisation Curriculum Development Project at Brandeis University, and draws heavily on Project material. The Study Group is grateful to Professor Perlman and his colleagues in the Project for their contribution.

community worker. No organisation is free from the constraints and pressures exerted by other organised groups in its environment. Their requirements and their influence or power – frequently based on legislation – will encourage or exclude actions by a community worker. Thus, for example, the willingness or ability of a decision-making body to contribute money and manpower will condition the actions of a community worker engaged in a project that requires new resources. By the same token, the values and cultural patterns of local people will also affect the tasks undertaken and methods employed by a community worker. To these various cross-currents must be added the influence of key individuals. At any given time there may be a difference between the problems and priorities as the worker sees them and as the group sees them. Bridging this gap is an essential skill in community work. There may not only be differences about priorities but the worker may also face difficulties in being accepted by the group and knowing how to communicate with it. There may also be differences of opinion within the group and between the group and the committee which it has appointed and the controlling body, which may either be appointed by the group itself or by a statutory or voluntary organisation providing a service to the community.

In brief, the employing organisation, the problem at hand and a variety of local pressures exert strong influences on the level and kind of action open to a community worker. This applies in all types of community work and whether the function is performed whole time or as part of another professional task.

To these circumstances and constraints must be added the ethical commitments and professional values of community workers discussed in the next chapter. These suggest certain ends and means and preclude others that are thought to be antisocial or destructive.

GENERAL PROBLEM-SOLVING FUNCTIONS

Much of the earlier writing on community work in the United States, Canada and this country stressed the various roles in which the worker is cast from time to time as an enabler, as a sustainer of morale, as an expert who provides information and advice and is skilled in community analysis, research and evaluation, or as a catalyst who improves communication, stimulates awareness of problems and motivates people to take action. Ross, Lippitt and others[1] have recognised that community workers shift from role to role according to circumstances.

1. Murray G. Ross with B. W. Lappin, *Community Organisation: Theory, Principles and Practice*, second edn., Harper & Row, 1967, p. 40; R. Lippitt, Jeanne Watson and Bruce Westley, *The Dynamics of Planned Change: A Comparative Study of Principles and Techniques*, Harcourt Brace, 1958, p. 312; T. R. Batten, *Communities and their Development*, Oxford University Press, 1957.

It is often suggested that the activities of community workers can also be understood as aspects or stages in the solving of problems. Writers differ in their terminology and in the number of steps they identify in problem-solving (for instance see Professor Marie Jahoda's analysis in a related context in chapter 9, p. 108). They do not always recognise the double task, i.e. definition of the problem by the worker and how he uses this to help the community to find its solution for itself. The analysis of the problem by the worker and by the community itself may well be different and to find the vital connecting link involves the essence of communication and skill in community work. The various stages in community problem solving can be fairly presented in this way:

1. Exploration and study of the situation and preliminary definition of a problem (or problems).
2. Creating structures and organisational arrangements to promote relationships and communication and developing formal machinery for study and action on problems.
3. Formulating policies and goals to guide action, after weighing alternatives and assessing what will be feasible.
4. Evaluation of intended and unintended consequences in order to make adjustments and to define new problems for study and action.

The activities of community workers contribute to one or more of these functions. A particular worker may concentrate on certain of these in accordance with the requirements of his job. Thus the worker with local groups may be heavily engaged for much of his time in the development of relationships and communication among people in an area as a prelude to discovering common problems, reaching agreement on them and acting accordingly. A community planner may devote a considerable proportion of his work to the study and analysis of problem situations. Nevertheless, the four-point scheme presented above makes it possible to place workers' activities in a framework that shows progression towards the accomplishment of a purpose, namely the identification and solution of a social problem.

It is not suggested that these functions are performed in a neat and tidy way in the order in which they are listed. Each is a continuous process, doubling back and crossing over the other processes and over itself. Thus fact finding and problem analysis go on, in most instances, until the final stages of a programme or project. Similarly, the worker is continually engaged in building lines of communication and promoting means of bringing people together and engaging them in active participation in the process.

One of the community worker's responsibilities is to see that these functions are effectively related to each other. For this purpose all the community worker's activities include both analysis and interaction with other people. Analysis consists of the collection and appropriate use of information, concepts and symbols, the preparation of alternative solutions to problems, and the worker's decisions about what action he will take. Interaction refers to contact, relationship and communication with others; giving and receiving information and opinions. It is a process of mutual influence whose purpose is to affect the course of some particular social change, guided by the needs and interests of the people concerned and within certain democratic value assumptions.

Analysis and interaction denote activities of the worker that supplement each other: they are inseparable and of equal importance. In fact, of course, they are simply abstract labels for two aspects of the worker's tasks. Analysis is directed toward finding rational solutions to social and organisational problems. But those solutions must inevitably be worked out in the market-place of the interests, needs and influence of many groups and organisations. The relations between the worker and these groups are essential to promote movement toward a goal. Interaction without careful thought, planning and evaluation would be pointless: analysis of a situation without fruitful relations with the people concerned would be sterile. The following is an attempt to clarify the processes in which both worker and group are engaged.

Phase	Analysis	Action
1. Exploration and study	Preliminary study and description of a situation. Assessing what opportunities and limits are imposed by the agency employing the practitioner and by other organisations.	Receiving and/or eliciting information and preferences from those experiencing the problem and other relevant persons. Communicating data to appropriate people.
2. Creating a structure and supports	Determining the nature of relationship with various people, means of communicating with them, and types of structure to be developed (committee, rota of volunteers, people for roles as experts, communicators, influencers, contributors, etc.).	Establishing formal and informal communications and recruiting participants for selected tasks and roles. Stimulating wider awareness of the problem, commitment to the organisation, etc.

Phase	*Analysis*	*Action*
3. Formulating policy	Postulating alternative goals, strategies, and resources. Selecting from among alternatives for recommendation to decision-makers in the light of resistances and opportunities.	Promoting expression and exchange of preferences. Testing out the feasibility of various alternatives with relevant persons. Assisting decision-makers to weigh alternatives, to choose, and to overcome resistances.
4. Implementing plans	Specifying in detail what tasks need to be performed to achieve the agreed goal, by whom, with what resources and procedures.	Agreeing plans with decision-makers and obtaining their commitments of resources. Putting the resources into action.
5. Evaluation	Designing a means for collecting, feeding back and analysing information on operations. Analysing consequences of change, specifying adjustments needed and/or new problems which call for action and planning.[1]	Obtaining data on operations.

It now remains to examine various types of community work. An effort will be made to describe functions and tasks in terms that are concrete and specific enough to suggest implications for training.

FACE-TO-FACE WORK WITH LOCAL GROUPS

The major function of community workers at the face-to-face or neighbourhood level is to organise and mobilise people for one or

1. Based upon the Community Organisation Curriculum Development Project's *Project Plan*, Council on Social Work Education, New York, 1965. For an analysis of the 'stages in the thinking process leading to action by a group', showing the interaction between the group and the worker, see T. R. Batten, *The Non-Directive Approach*, p. 47.

more of these purposes: (1) to help them to make better use of existing services; (2) to implement self help activities; (3) to press for changes in the policies of established organisations, principally those providing social services.

The worker must continually obtain, study and analyse demographic, social, cultural and economic data relating to the locality in which he works so that he is able to relate these to specific events and interpret them in their total context. This provides the basis for the formation of local groups and the encouragement of voluntary action to agree upon and meet particular needs, as far as such action lies within their competence. His role is also concerned with problems of communication.

Thus his function is to clarify priorities of social need by fact finding and by encouraging members of the community to consider their own problems and attempt to relate these to other available services. He offers to groups in the community information which will educate, inform and enable them to perceive more accurately the nature of their own problems in relation to the commitments, obligations, and limitations of the organisations and resources which they can call upon. It is clear that in encouraging members of the community to discuss their problems, in educating them as to the nature of these and in helping them to take action on their own behalf, the community worker may become engaged in political activity. This is discussed from different angles in chapters 3 and 7.

An illustration of the full time community worker in face-to-face contact with local groups is provided by a project in an economically depressed and physically deteriorated part of a large English city which is concentrating its efforts in a small area of overcrowded housing, where rents are high but amenities and community facilities reflect the general poverty of the area. Side by side with widespread apathy go violence and antisocial activities. The goals of the project are the promotion of self help activities, the modification of existing services and the establishment of new ones by statutory and voluntary agencies. The project is directed towards influencing two sections of the community: the unorganised residents and the organised agencies and groups in the community.

Clearly it is important for the community worker to learn about the area in which he will be working. However, even before he begins to study the area he and his employing organisation must decide how the study is to be conducted, who is to be involved from among the residents, local groups, associations, statutory and voluntary service organisations; and in what ways and through what structures they are to be involved. The purpose of the study is to compile a profile of the area, its physical, social and economic characteristics, the needs and problems of the people, and the adequacy or limitations of existing provisions and services. These first steps would be much the same for a worker who had been given a more narrowly defined task to stimulate a better provision for a part of the population, e.g. the aged, the handicapped, or young people.

Such a reconnaissance of a neighbourhood (or of a specific community problem) calls upon skills and methods that have been developed by social scientists and researchers. Unlike the scientist the community worker must use information as a basis for action rather than for knowledge and understanding as ends in themselves. Thus in the course of studying the local situation the community worker forms groups and opens up channels of communication with a view to helping people to assume responsibility for defining problems, examining alternative approaches, and selecting goals and policies. It is here that an understanding of social structures and cultural norms and values is important in selecting the appropriate groups to engage in the study phase. The actual involvement of people in fact finding, discussion of findings and opinions, and in reaching decisions about policies and action draws upon another set of skills and methods that have been developed by those who work with small groups for educational, recreational or therapeutic purposes. An understanding of group relationships and dynamics, inter-group tensions and social pressures is essential for community work.

The community worker will arrive at his own analysis or definition of the situation during the study period. His next task is to select the goals and means that seem likely to be most effective. He must then decide how to present his deductions to the group or groups making decisions, e.g. whether to indicate a single or alternative course of action, with or without recommendations.

The result of the study and policy formulation phases is decision about a line of action. The main types of action are listed below, with emphasis on the worker's function:

Disseminating information in the community.

Influencing or assisting people to use available resources; helping them to obtain their full rights to existing services.

Starting new organisations or strengthening existing ones, primarily by recruiting new members into the association.

Training people in leadership skills, in organisation operations, in the processes of thinking and acting together in problem-solving.

Helping people to organise a new project or service on a self help basis.

Helping people to take collective action either as a means of enhancing their self-esteem, improving their living conditions, or for social control.

It will be apparent that many of these tasks, far from being mutually exclusive, are often pursued simultaneously, so that it is

71

frequently difficult to see which are ends and which are means. Each line of action calls upon the worker to use knowledge and skills appropriate to the task, whether it be, for example, the preparation of educational materials or the training of leaders.

Quite often a worker at this level enters a situation with his task already defined. Thus a welfare department may think it important to interpret its services locally and to educate people to use them; or a community worker may concentrate on training volunteers to carry out their tasks more effectively.

The community worker must not only implement a plan but also provide for observation and criticism as a basis for modifying and strengthening it. Here again social research methods are relevant to the selection of persons and methods best suited to continuous evaluations and improvement of a given piece of community work.[1]

DEVELOPING AND COORDINATING SERVICES

Community work functions at this middle level consist of improving, coordinating and developing services within and among organisations in the local community. In this context 'organisations' include (1) those that provide direct services, (2) those that determine policies and allocate resources for the provision of services, and (3) those representing the consumers of services and other interests in the community. Our concern here is with the professional functions performed by persons in these organisations, with much of the responsibility falling to workers in direct service organisations. Our focus on these functions and on the climate within which they are carried out is well illustrated by D. V. Donnison in *Social Policy and Administration:*

> Development and change – not stability and equilibrium – are the dominant features of the social services. The evolution of these services is not an impersonal or automatic response to the external pressures of supply and demand, neither is it simply dictated by legislation; it is largely brought about by the people who work in the services. How do these services develop? How do new services begin, how do changes come about in the scope and character of existing services, why do such changes take place, and what parts are played in this process by different people, different interests and different groups?[2]

1. See for example, Peter Kuenstler, *Community Organisation in Great Britain*, Faber, 1961; *Working with Communities*, National Council of Social Service, 1963, and *Community Organisation Work in Progress*, National Council of Social Service, 1965.

2. D. V. Donnison, *Social Policy and Administration*, Allen & Unwin, 1965, p. 29.

Donnison is concerned with those processes 'which bring about changes in the volume, character or distribution of the services provided by local units of the social services. These agencies may be voluntary or statutory, national or local.'[1]

The main tasks involved in bringing about such changes consist of studies of the effectiveness of existing services in the light of changing social conditions; development of new patterns of inter-organisational cooperation in the provision of services, or of new services; improvement in communication between providers and users of services.

The use of research methods in the analysis and study of services is a crucial task here as elsewhere. Much of the work consists of writing reports and proposals, the establishment of committees and working parties and providing them with information and recommendations; and negotiating the acquisition of additional resources to implement a scheme for new or expanded services. These activities are also important in other kinds of community work.

A substantial part of the work entails obtaining new resources. This demands that administrator-planners should analyse the possibilities and then test them out with those who control money, manpower and other resources. Some of the issues and strategies inherent in performing these tasks are essential in community work but certainly not confined to it. They are indeed a generalised function in many organisational or inter-organisational situations in a state of change.

The initiation and execution of the kind of changes described by Donnison often require the participation of organisations and individuals across a wide front, extending far beyond the providing group. Thus, a group of consumers such as a tenants' association or parents of mentally handicapped children, or a coordinating body such as a council of social service may call attention to a growing social problem and thereby give the initial impetus to the processes of study, policy-determination and implementation of some new service.

Another responsibility relates to the creation and maintenance of horizontal channels of communication to enable members of different professions to relate their work to that of their colleagues, and also to broad aspects of local community life. Thus at different levels of organisation the official with a community perspective would have particular responsibility in relation to executive or policy-making teams; within these teams leadership roles would change with the changing priorities for action but the responsibility for ensuring that the teams meet, and discharge their purpose competently, would need to be clearly defined. In some circumstances

1. *Ibid.*, p. 231.

the community worker might have administrative responsibilities as coordinator: in others he might act as a consultant.

Attempts to achieve horizontal communication and to obtain a flow of information which will override the divisions between professions and services are of course numerous, but the degree to which such attempts succeed or fail depends on the degree to which constituent members feel themselves committed to a given coordinating activity, and whether they regard the jointly defined objectives as binding upon them.[1] The aim should be to devise policies that take account of the needs and desires of the people served in relation to available resources. The Report of the Maud Committee[2] discusses in detail the extent and manner in which organisational structure affects coordination in the provision of services in local government.

NATIONAL, REGIONAL AND LOCAL PLANNING

Various community or social planning functions are performed not only at the local but also at national and regional levels by people in a wide range of governmental and voluntary organisations. The essence of their work is research, planning, policy-formulation and implementation, though most of their job titles do not indicate that these are their full time or main duties.

At this level community work in its broadest form may contribute an element in comprehensive physical-economic-social planning for a region of the country. Or it may be directed to long-range planning on a national basis to meet particular needs, for instance the needs of the physically handicapped or the aged. More often, however, social planning efforts have a more restricted and immediate focus on some gap or dislocation that has been identified in the way needs are being met.

Often the planner's first task is the collection and analysis of information that bears on the problem under review. He must also be concerned about participation from other organisations. Which interests ought to be represented at the outset? Which can be brought in later? These are the kind of questions that a planner must cope with, quite apart from the technical and methodological research issues he faces. Knowledge of the formal and informal operations of government and voluntary organisations at the national level is essential to making sound decisions on these questions. This includes bringing together for a common purpose other organisations with differing interests and with varied professional preoccupations. The planner's task in this aspect of his total function is to help to clarify

1. See R. L. Warren, *Types of Purposive Social Change at the Community Level*, no. 11, Papers in Social Welfare, Brandeis University, Massachusetts, 1965.
2. *Management of Local Government*, 1967.

essential issues and to enable all concerned to make realistic policy decisions capable of being implemented.

It is naïve to think that all planning and policy development begins with a blank sheet and a need or desire for data. Accumulated experience of a particular service or of political pressures may provide valid guides for a planner to begin at the point of constructing and weighing alternative means of reaching a solution that has already been accepted in principle. Thus, for example, a decision may have already been taken to bring about improved coordination of services between two agencies; the question posed for the planner is how this is to be achieved.

Much of the work at this level consists of analytical tasks. Indeed many jobs are devoted entirely to this. The skills and many of the tasks have much in common with those of the social scientist searching for explanatory factors in a situation; the planner is trying to answer such questions as why are there increasing numbers of people who suffer from this disability or disadvantage and what can be done to rehabilitate them and to prevent others from joining their ranks.

When the planner has probed causal connections and decided on a strategy, he turns his attention to designing interventions. His task now calls for a combination of the expertise of an administrator and the knowledge and skill of a professional familiar with a particular problem or service. Understanding of the content, the strengths and the limitations of current practice is important to planning, whether the field is child care, services to the handicapped, or the rehousing of people displaced by urban renewal. This understanding, combined with skill in management, must be available – either in the person of the planner or among his colleagues – so that he can specify what resources of money and staff and what techniques and procedures will be required to mount the service he is proposing. He must be able to say where they can be obtained and how they should be disposed. In one sense these are technical questions, and the planner's function is to cope with them in rational ways. (It should be noted that the functions described here are frequently performed by the administrator himself, often in concert with others on his staff.)

Many policy decisions can only be made by elected representatives. But the formulation and implementation of policy confronts the community planner with the task of helping to resolve certain political problems. 'Political' is used here in its broadest meaning to refer to policy considerations. For example, the planner must know not only where resources may be found, but how they can be obtained for the purpose he has in mind. Planning at this level must therefore be informed by knowledge of resources, policies, interests and organisational patterns of institutions operating at the national, regional and local levels, because all these enter into the formulation and implementation of feasible policies. This is especially important in view of the fact that the community planner at the regional or national level is often faced with the fact that real control is exercised locally, and that only through a sensitive understanding of local conditions, needs and problems can he assist or persuade local authorities to improve and extend their services, even when central government resources are available, and to make provision for maximum participation by voluntary organisations and self help groups in the operation of these services in the life of the community generally.

The social or community planning function as such does not include the actual operation of a service. This is in itself an administrative task. The planner is concerned with marshalling resources, with designing methods of evaluating a new service, so that, as a matter of routine, information will be collected on its operations. It is an essential planning function continually to collect, analyse and interpret data and present findings and recommendations for adjustments and changes, both in the operation of services and in basic policies. These separate functions may or may not be performed by the same persons. Where they are combined in one person routine administration may oust the planning function.

CONCLUSION

It has been implied throughout these observations that the various elements in community work are intimately linked to each other and that the training of workers ought to make these connections explicit and to give those in training some basic understanding of each.

In an attempt to clarify in an orderly way the stages or processes in the functions and tasks of community workers, we have inevitably not analysed in similar detail the reactions of groups or individuals at various stages and according to their degree of motivation, their perception of their problems and their ability to work together for agreed ends.

It is essential for community workers to be skilled, not only at motivating people to come together initially, but also at supporting them through the stages of decision making and implementation when conflict about aims and methods, and disappointment with slow progress, may otherwise result in projects being abandoned or the participants losing heart and a sense of purpose. Community workers will not succeed unless they are able to live with conflict and tension, as well as being able to recognise and handle problems of power politics.

7

Values and Objectives in Community Work

All interventions in social affairs, whether by a statutory or voluntary agency, raise questions of the authority – legal, financial, social and ultimately moral – for such interventions. On whose behalf are they made? With what right and with what objective? With what safe-guards against abuse? What ills are they intended to cure? By whom and how are priorities determined? Where do they succeed or fail? These questions about social betterment can only be given answers in terms of values.

Both the questions and the decisions about priorities and social responsibility which they pose come back in the last resort to attempts to promote change for the better. This is a controversial concept when it passes beyond saying that health is 'better' than sickness or education than ignorance. Not only do people's values, whether choices or moral imperatives, differ, but values themselves may conflict with each other, and limited resources usually compel choices between them. To say that the aim of community work is the wellbeing and development of the individual human person as a member of a community is certainly to state an ultimate criterion, to rule out some activities and add weight to others. But instrumental values and the pragmatic test are essential for day-to-day purposes. These instrumental values include better opportunities for choice and its responsible exercise; enabling people of different ages to engage in richer and more varied relationships with others; bringing about a more satisfactory balance between individual needs and social demands; making it possible for the individual to experience freedom and initiative in a bureaucratic, technological society. These are all value laden terms which can only be put to the test in actual situations where limited resources, conflict of interests, negative feelings about deviant or minority groups, and large-scale organisa-tion, apathy or self-interest, may restrict 'ideal' solutions.

These are crucial questions of social values in an open, complex and rapidly changing society. All community work is shot through with assumptions that some forms of social life and social change are 'better' than others. It is important at least to be aware of such assumptions and not to stress the unity and harmony of community work at the expense of recognising the equally valid aspects of competition and conflict that stem from differences in needs, values and outlook. Much of this work is concerned with the necessity for adjustments between different interest groups, some more powerful than others and each convinced of the legitimacy of its particular demands for attention or for limited resources.

THE UNDERLYING VALUES

Community work is rooted in certain beliefs which derive from our culture and society and are shared with a number of helping professions and reforming activities. Basically they are concerned with ideas about human worth and human betterment. Different people express them in different ways and with varying emphases, but at a broad level of generality or vagueness there is considerable overlap. Various lists include the dignity and worth of the individual; freedom to express individuality; the right to a decent standard of living; the right to struggle for social improvements; the superiority of self-induced change over imposed change; cooperation and integration among community groups; the community's capacity to solve problems; the human control of the natural and social environment through the planning of changes in the function and structure of social units and of society as a whole with the purpose of improving the relationship of people to their environment and strengthening their ability to cope with change in the future. Other analyses include improvements in conditions of social welfare and in man's capacity to cope with social problems; and national planning based on knowledge of cause-effect relationships as superior to other methods of solving problems, particularly in terms of economising the time and resources of the planner and his organisation.[1] Biddle suggests that community development 'should help the participants to achieve a more meaningful existence, to become more responsive to human

1. See for example:
Murray G. Ross with B. W. Lappin, *Community Organisation: Theory, Principles and Practice* (second edn.), Harper and Row, New York, 1967.
Ronald Lippitt and others, *The Dynamics of Planned Change*, Harcourt Brace, New York, 1958.
Robert Morris and Robert H. Binstock, *Feasible Planning for Social Change*, Columbia University Press, 1966.
Graham Lomas, ed., *Social Aspects of Urban Development*, National Council of Social Service, 1966.
E. B. Harper and A. Dunham, *Community Organisation in Action*, Association Press, New York, 1959.
Harry L. Lurie, *The Community Organisation Method in Social Work Education*, Council for Social Work Education, New York, 1959.
Raymond T. Clarke, *Working with Communities*, National Council of Social Service, 1963.
Eileen Younghusband, *Social Work and Social Change*, Allen & Unwin, 1964.
R. A. B. Leaper, *Communities and Social Change*, National Council of Social Service, 1963, and *Community Work*, National Council of Social Service, 1968, chapter 4.

needs, and to become more competent to live harmoniously with neighbours.'[1]

These values summarised
In the simplest terms, the values with which community work is ultimately concerned may be stated in the form of the following propositions:

1. That a democratic society exists to enable all its citizens to develop their various talents and interests to the fullest possible extent. The concern is with the wholeness of man and his ultimate value by virtue of his humanity.

2. That much of the individual's capacity for growth and development depends on his active association with his fellows in a number of different groups. Man is a social animal and it is only through living in society that he survives, communicates and shares in a culture. Hence the community in which he lives profoundly affects his development. It is from participating and sharing in social, economic, occupational, political and religious activities that individuals gain their friendships, find their identity and are able to give to as well as take from their society.

3. That respect for another individual must include respect for his beliefs, his ability to reach decisions and to build his own life. Variety in a society is a good to be welcomed in its own right.

4. That society thrives on the interplay between leadership, organisation and freedom, though few can suggest what the right balance is between organisation from above and development from below. Moreover, in an increasingly technological, complex society this balance is constantly shifting, with increasing constriction on freedom of choice in some directions and greater opportunities in others.

THE RELATIONS BETWEEN SOCIETY AND THE INDIVIDUAL

If we accept these propositions or similar ones it follows that community activity is not only a means to a particular end (e.g. the development of social opportunities) but is also a means for making more possible the richer and more diverse expression of all that we regard as best in the personality. Overdependence on outside authority, alienation from one's fellows, self-centred striving, are likely to lead to impoverishment of personality. It also follows that there needs to be a range of community activities with differing purposes and degree of involvement. There will certainly be conflict, but this will often add spice rather than vinegar to life. The central

1. William W. Biddle and L. J. Biddle, *The Community Development Process*, Holt, Rinehart and Winston, 1966, p. 231.

characteristic, however, if our concern is with human personality, must be promotion of personal relationships and with creating the conditions which make it easier for people to form relationships with others. It is through relationships that human beings express themselves and from relationships draw their deepest satisfactions.

Through membership of different groups the individual finds security for himself in being accepted as a person by other persons whom he knows, the relationships with whom give him guidance about how to manage his own impulses, and solidarity with whom gives him significance in face of external changes and chances. In mobile societies community development means seeking to help individuals at the mercy of the outside world to discover, define, pursue and achieve common objectives, and in the process to develop more confident relationships with one another and the outside world. The essence of community work is an effort to relate factors making for change in society to the inherent general needs of persons including their need for stable and congenial relationships with other persons. In pursuit of this general goal it may often be necessary to help people to press for such practical aids to wellbeing as better housing, better working conditions, and higher standards of living.

There are major social factors operating against the maintenance of stable and congenial relationships between persons, and one must therefore consider why relationships of this sort matter. It cannot be taken as self-evident that membership of a community is a good thing, even though it is a matter of empirical observation that, in human society, the willing isolate is unusual. Given the confusion and incoherence of individual propensities, the individual who has no 'feeling' relationship with an identifiable group of other people has no way of testing the meaning of his impulses, interpretations and interests. The larger society will subject him to legal control, but it operates at long range, is clumsy, undiscriminating, and tends to react formatively only in face of outrage. It is as 'felt' members of interdependent communities that persons experience social control with relatively little fuss, relatively little tension and maximum informality, gaining thereby within themselves knowledge of the measure of conformity expected of them and in what directions and how far they may exercise divergent initiative.

A society is healthier for a wide diffusion among its members of the experience of friendship in some depth, and where this is made difficult for particular people society is to that extent the loser through the emotional impoverishment of its members. In societies which are economically, technologically and politically sophisticated in the sense that they conceive and organise change, the individual is the object of manipulation by those who possess organised powers of persuasion or compulsion. Exercise of centralised power without regard for its social consequences may contribute to the social disorientation of individuals. Alternatively, change may open the way for new relationships and for new forms of community experience. What matters is the extent to which the individual, or individuals, feel themselves able to face the pressures of the outside world with the support of other people similarly affected. Because there are large impersonal forces at work in society making for rapid change, it is important that men and women should feel that account is also taken of them as persons – though, of course, few of them would make the point in this generalised conceptual form.

It is important, too, that community workers should not find themselves in the position of opposing change almost as a matter of conviction. It may well be their job to promote change and in any event to see that considerations based on the value of persons as persons should not be neglected in the process of change. And they should perceive the ways in which change gives the individual the opportunity of making more satisfying choices and should help individuals to press for the building in of these opportunities as change takes place, rather than chasing after the change in order to introduce remedial action.

VALUES RELATED TO PRACTICE

A recent intercultural seminar of social scientists and social work educators focused on two complementary sets of values: the worth and dignity of man related to the wellbeing and integrity of the group and the progress and development of the individual as related to the security of the individual and society. It was suggested that these

may in the absence of evidence to the contrary, be thought of as universal values, from the standpoint of social welfare and social work. One or other of each pair may be dominant in a given society at a given time, but it seems most unlikely that any society will ever be found in which both members of either pair are completely lacking in the psychology of individuals, as values of the total society, or of segments of it.[1]

When these very general formulations were considered in relation to actual practice, a number of issues arose which are typically expressed in dichotomous form – stability and change, conservation and innovation, competition and cooperation, conflict and consensus, participation and expertism, individual or community self help and social services, ends and means, and so on.

From the standpoint of the worker the question is 'to what extent

1. *An Intercultural Exploration: Universals and Differences in Social Work Values: Functions and Practice*, Report of the Intercultural Seminar held at the East–West Center, Hawaii, 1966, Council on Social Work Education, New York, 1967, p. 17.

he should be directive, in the sense of making proposals offering definite plans of action, advocating these plans of action, and seeking to persuade other people to agree and to support them; or to what extent should he seek rather to help people formulate their own objectives, as one step in a long process of learning how to make more effective decisions together'.[1]

Although these two approaches can be theoretically distinguished, in the practice of community work they are closely related. At any given time or in any particular situation one or the other may have priority but neither should be pursued exclusively. This persistent tension and interrelation between task and process in community work is to some extent paralleled by the distinction between analytic and interaction skills in community work practice.

The American National Association of Social Workers suggests that in the practice of community work attempts should be made to realise values by making the following assumptions:

1. Changes in which individuals, groups and organisations determine their own destiny in a democratic process have a better chance of enduring than changes which are imposed.
2. Readiness for change is a variable which affects the potential and the rate of community change obtainable at any given time.
3. Skills in participating in a democratic process can be taught and learned by individuals and groups.
4. Society can provide ways to achieve maximum compatibility of individual and community interests.
5. Social welfare provisions, services and programmes can enhance human welfare and prevent and reduce social ills.
6. Planning, coordination and integration of social welfare provision, services and programmes, governmental, private and voluntary, is necessary; human welfare is indivisible; social ills are interrelated; and social welfare provision, services and programmes are interdependent.[2]

PROFESSIONAL ETHICS

Community workers not only need concern for people and scientifically based working methods, but also a combination of concern and objectivity coupled with personal integrity. Different groups or members of a group will try to involve them in getting things for them, favouring one group against another, or supporting unrealistic projects or solutions. They will also often find themselves caught between pressures to take one side against another, and to bring political pressure to bear either to press the community's demands or

1. *Ibid.*, p. 74.
2. *Defining Community Organisation Practice*, N.A.S.W., New York, 1962, p. 7.

to resist them. They may also incur disfavour for expressing the needs of a deviant group.[1]

Apart from pressure to take sides, they will inevitably be 'for' some things and 'against' others, for tolerance and against discrimination, for adventure playgrounds and against asphalt, for example. They will also sometimes find themselves ineffective because they are outside a power system, or too low in a hierarchical organisation, or caught between different pressure groups in a conflict of power politics. They are subject to the tensions inherent in professional practice from within bureaucratic organisations. And, as has been said in earlier chapters, their work may quickly have political implications. Thus community workers often face acute tensions of loyalty to the people they serve. To make people more aware of their needs and more vocal about them may stir up trouble which can lead to expressions in forms more violent than wise. Community workers need great integrity and judgement not to be caught between the cross-fire that results, but on the contrary to help each side to see the other's point of view. If this is not possible, in the last resort the community worker must decide whether he should either resign or compromise.

THE COMMUNITY WORKER'S OWN VALUES[2]

The values of the community worker, whatever their origin, have an all-pervading influence on his work and deserve close examination. They represent indeed a means of implementing society's decisions as to ways of handling certain forms of individual, group and community behaviour and thus are deeply concerned with the cultural values of society. Although it is possible to identify certain basic values which most people in this country would acknowledge, for example democratic political values, it is easy to show that within an overall homogeneity there exists a diversity of values which has its roots in community, social class and ethnic differences. Individuals are not born into the total culture of any society, but into a matrix of subcultures which reflect the community, class and ethnic position which the family occupies in the social structure. These subcultures carry with them systems of values which the child learns through the agency of the family and other social institutions.

The diversity of values in society has important implications for community work. It means that the community worker must recognise that he is himself the product of a particular subculture which may have a value system at variance with that of the

1. For an example of this see the reactions of local people to group work with acting out adolescents in Spencer, *Stress and Release in an Urban Estate*, pp. 202–15.

2. This section to the end of the chapter is largely based on material in an unpublished article by Peter Leonard. The Study Group is indebted to him for permission to use it.

community in which he is doing his professional work. Whether the community worker is consciously abiding by or rebelling against the values of his own upbringing or is identified with a set of professional values, they will all influence him and require conscious perception especially when he is working in a community with different cultural traditions from his own. 'All social workers should be expected to be critical of their own irrationality, not only in terms of psychology, but also in terms of the cultural origins of their values and the structural pressures which in any particular social position tend to reinforce them.'[1] Diversity of values also means that social problems within communities are perceived differently by different sections of the community and ideas on the allocation of responsibility for solving such problems may also differ.

THE LIMITATIONS OF SELF-DETERMINATION

Community work may be seen as one of the means by which society induces individuals and groups to modify their behaviour in the direction of certain cultural norms. Such a formulation of the goals of community work, so far as society is concerned, might be rejected by many community workers, and stress placed instead upon helping communities to find their own solutions to problems. However, community self-determination has certain limits, for there are some kinds of community behaviour, such as racial intolerance, or local patterns of delinquent behaviour, which community workers would aim to eliminate in the light of values which may lie outside the community itself, even though this might go against the wishes of many people in the locality.

In community work it is assumed that the worker's positive feelings of acceptance and goodwill towards the community are necessary in any help that is to be given, and the aim of community work is to increase tolerance, good neighbourliness and social responsibility, and to decrease intolerance, prejudice and fear. The problem is that the community worker may come to confuse what is with what ought to be, and through fear of arousing hostility in the community, deny the reality of this distinction. Yet there are many conflicting interests (even at the neighbourhood level) and, as has been said, each group presses its claim to goods, services and status, and each is convinced of the legitimacy of its demands. Much community work is concerned with deciding when there is need for adjustment and accommodation among these interest groups or when the claims of some less powerful group with pressing problems should be given priority and actively supported.

The community worker attempts to broaden and deepen the com-

1. Communication to the Study Group from Professor Paul Stirling, University of Kent, 1967.

munity's understanding of its own general problems and those of particular groups. This, though apparently slower than telling people what they need and how to achieve it, an approach which they frequently reject, is assumed in the long run to be more effective, and to help self-development and self-determination. The values to which we referred on pp. 78–9 imply that rights are based upon the individual rather than upon the group or upon status and that there should be no discrimination between races, nationalities, rich or poor, educated or uneducated, clean or dirty, 'deserving' or 'undeserving' in the quality of the services provided by the community worker. In practice, of course, community workers, like others, may have their own prejudices which, unless faced, may lead them to discriminate against some deviant individuals or groups in the interests of the community as a whole. This is different from deciding who must be supported in an ultimate conflict of interests (see p. 83). Community workers may also face personal conflicts between professional values and other loyalties.

Belief in the value of diversity in human life lies, of course, at the base of the idea of self-determination in social work. We have noted already that society will only allow diversity to proceed so far, and that beyond a certain point conformity is required. Nevertheless, within these limits, the ideal of self-determination provides the community worker with the moral imperative not to strive for uniformity, to help the community, within limits, to fashion its own solutions to problems rather than follow stereotypes of 'good community life' which may be in the mind of the community worker. But this is no answer to the problem of determining whether the community worker should express his own values or only let local people express theirs – in the hope that his and their values will in time converge.

There are further limitations on community self-determination which should be considered. The community worker may be, or may seem to be, in a position to influence and change the social environment and so be accorded a deference which leads to an over-ready acceptance of his ideas or his authority. The community worker does not exist in a social and political vacuum but, whether employed by a statutory or a voluntary body, may be under pressure from powerful local interests to prevent any challenge to the *status quo*, and to strive for conformity to bureaucratic needs. Moreover, it is not always clear in a variety of group and intergroup situations who or what is the 'self' that determines or, indeed, who is the 'client' and who has the right to be supported.

WHO KNOWS BEST ?

There is a temptation, both in the community worker and his employing organisation, to assume that communities require reorientation to bring them into line with certain stereotypes of community and family life, stereotypes which often reflect particular class assumptions.

The implications for the community worker of class-linked attitudes to education and to the distribution of roles within the family, attitudes which reflect value differences, are also of considerable importance. The community worker needs to be fully aware of his own class-linked values in the field of education, family relationships and community interaction, for he may tend to assume, unthinkingly, that his own values are in the last resort more right or more natural than those of others. Community workers and their employing organisations have a responsibility to make conscious decisions about the social changes and cultural values they wish to encourage, and what are the ethical constraints and imperatives in influencing people so as to bring about social change and what constitutes desirable social change. Self-awareness and understanding of value assumptions is obviously an important element in training for community work (see chapters 9, pp. 112–113, 10, p. 123, and 11, p. 135).

PART THREE

Training

8

Patterns of Training

PRIORITIES AND THE NEED FOR A COHERENT PATTERN OF
TRAINING

The Study Group's primary task was to examine community work in this country with a view to making proposals about training. Having clarified the functions and tasks outlined in chapters 3 and 5, the next steps are to fit training for community work into existing training structures and to outline its content. Those for whom provision must be made include existing full time community workers, new entrants, other professionals with a community work element in their functions, and voluntary workers.

Plans for training must take account of priorities. There are many people engaged in community work of one kind or another who have had no training for it, yet who urgently need to understand better the nature of the task and the knowledge, attitudes and skills which it involves. Thus in-service training of all kinds is a high priority. Much is already happening here, but much more needs to be done. In-service training is discussed later in this chapter (pp. 99–100). In any comprehensive planning it is essential for employing authorities to recognise that in the present dearth of qualified workers in-service training is the most realistic way of improving performance and creating a climate favourable to community work methods and to full time professional training.

It is equally necessary to expand the very limited amount of full time training available at the present time. Real advances in practice will only come about from such training and the pressure it exerts on those who teach students, whether in the classroom or fieldwork, to relate theoretical knowledge to practice. None the less we advocate a quick expansion of in-service training and a slow expansion of full time courses. In view of this it may seem paradoxical that we devote so much attention to the latter. This is because ways of providing in-service training and its various patterns are well defined, whereas courses to qualify students for community work are not. Moreover, in-service training in its nature can only contain some part of what should be studied more adequately in longer courses. Therefore when we come to the content of training in chapters 9, 10 and 11 we shall present its desirable range in the light of present knowledge, leaving selection of the content for any particular course to be decided according to its relevance for inclusion in other professional courses, casework or teaching, for example, or in various general or specific in-service training courses.

We hope that the Aves Committee[1] will cast new light on aspects of the training and use of volunteers that are outside our own terms of reference. There is also a valuable study of the training and needs of volunteers in the second *Report of the Working Party on the Place of Voluntary Service in After-Care* (the Reading Report).[2]

PROFESSIONAL TRAINING FOR FULL TIME COMMUNITY
    WORK

As we have already said in chapter 4, in our view community work will only attract the right candidates if a career structure and training worthy of its potentialities and responsibilities are developed. Training for community centre wardens and for the youth service started with high hopes in the early 1940s but has failed to gain a real foothold during the ensuing years. This is due to various causes. One of these is undoubtedly that both the training and career structure are fragmented and limited instead of being part of the whole body of social work, further education, or administration. This experience has important implications for community work training. At present, as we have pointed out, a few appointments are being made in each of a variety of services to do essentially similar jobs. Until these are recognised as community work and a proper career structure created it is idle to hope that good candidates will be forthcoming or that hard-pressed universities and other educational institutions will invest scarce resources in pioneering sound professional training for community work in various settings. Inevitably the pattern of training for community work must be related to the bewildering variety of training for related professions in various educational institutions in this country at the present time. This means allowing for various ways of covering the necessary basic studies.

For example, existing applied social studies courses usually last for one year, following a degree or diploma in social studies. A separate community work stream or option might well be developed within the ambit of such a course. The evidence in chapter 5 shows that a limited amount of teaching about community work is beginning to be introduced into some existing casework courses. This is likely to be extended so that casework students will have some understanding and limited experience of group and community work. If

1. The Committee on Voluntary Workers in the Social Services, Chairman, Miss G. M. Aves, C.B.E. An independent committee of enquiry set up by the National Council of Social Service and the National Institute for Social Work Training. Its report is due in 1969.

2. H.M.S.O., 1967 (there is a reference to the Gulbenkian Study Group on p. 10).

the aim is also to give students real competence in work with groups or communities, then it is likely that the courses would have to be lengthened to two years or more following a university social studies qualification, or longer for other courses.

Most of the existing university applied social studies courses for graduates in other subjects are being lengthened from seventeen months to two years. There are signs that in due time these will include a parallel community work stream.

The new four-year 'integrated' degree courses, whether degrees conferred by the Council for National Academic Awards or on the lines of those at the Universities of Bath, Bradford and Keele, are to be welcomed, since their first two years of common basic studies followed by two years of professional preparation will facilitate later transfer from one career to another after a year or more of further professional preparation. Some of these degrees are likely to include qualifications for teaching, administration or personnel management as well as casework. The addition of a similar qualification for community work would make a particularly desirable pattern.

The largest single source of recruitment to casework at the present time comes from the two-year child care and certificate in social work courses in colleges of further education and university extramural departments. Many of these include some teaching about community care. We hope that in time parallel courses in community work will also be offered, in close association and sharing some teaching with the casework courses. As we have said above, in relation to university courses, these may ultimately be lengthened to become courses in social work, using all three methods of work with individuals, groups and communities, rather than casework alone.

Some community work, for example in community centres or the youth service, is an amalgamation of informal education and community development. The courses already pioneered in several colleges of education and at the National College for the Training of Youth Leaders have an important place within the general pattern which we outline in this chapter.

So far we have spoken of candidates without a related qualification who are starting to train as professional community workers; some of these will already have relevant experience and a number may be seconded by their employing authority for training.

Teachers, youth leaders and caseworkers with a professional qualification, and others with certain qualifications in administration, should, at least for the time being, be permitted to qualify for community work by means of a specially designed one-year course. Special measures would also be necessary in the early stages for the experienced but unqualified, and we suggest that those with substantial experience in community work should be permitted to take a one-year course designed to meet their needs.

So far as youth leadership is concerned, there are those who think that a training for community work with emphasis on the needs of young people would be more appropriate than the present pattern.

We hope that those who hold a professional qualification in community work would be enabled to transfer with say an additional year of training to another form of social work or to teaching, and would be recognised as qualified youth leaders.

We think that adult education techniques and management studies as well as social work have important elements to contribute to community work. None the less, the primary underpinning of knowledge comes from the social and behavioural sciences. Thus in our view professional education for community work should be located in university social study or adult education departments and certain colleges of further and higher education with substantial whole or part-time teaching resources in the social sciences. Inevitably these departments would also draw on the contribution of others, especially for teaching about adult education methods, the theory and techniques of communication, some aspects of management studies, social philosophy and political theory.

Before we leave the question of full time training for community work, we must consider the very difficult question of whether those engaged in direct community development need the same training as those who will operate at an inter-agency, organisational level, either in a particular locality or regionally. It is arguable that these are often different kinds of people with a different outlook and aptitudes. The successful worker with unattached youth or grossly deprived people living in substandard conditions is not necessarily a good administrator nor skilful at planning and carrying through larger social strategies. Moreover, when it comes to the actual content of the training that would enable each of them to do a better job, some of the knowledge will be different, they will not always make the same use of the same knowledge, and their fieldwork practice will have differences as well as similarities. There is also the question of age: quite young as well as older people can undoubtedly succeed in some direct community work, provided they are given constant support. Fairly senior posts at a local or regional level call, on the other hand, for longer experience as well as familiarity with bureaucratic structures. This suggests not only that the actual content of training will differ in some respects for the different types of community work but also that the point of entry to employment will also depend upon whether or not the student has experience and relevant professional qualifications.

Nonetheless, all community workers must possess skill in the analysis of a social situation, in group and intergroup relations and with individuals, who often have conflicting interests and points of view. They must also know about and cooperate with the local statutory and voluntary social services and part of their task in working with local people is to make the authorities more aware of their needs and of acceptable ways of meeting these. It must also be remembered that many community workers are employed to combine various elements of community work as defined in chapter 3, pp. 34–5, in their activities. In any event, we do not envisage the field-worker being unattached in the sense that he has no organisation behind him; indeed experience shows that he needs considerable consultative and other support. This probably means that training should qualify community workers both for direct neighbourhood and inter-agency work. In our view it is desirable that to the greatest extent possible there should be a common training, no matter what the diversity of organisational patterns, although it may sometimes be necessary to have different streams or options within the same course.

We do not think that community work which is intended to meet the needs of particular groups, the handicapped or immigrants for example, changes its essential nature. The situation may be rather different in the youth service and community centres where informal education skills are possibly needed to a greater extent.

As community work develops, there will be demands for further and advanced training. This advanced training for consultants, for those in senior posts, or those specialising in some particularly difficult aspect of the work will only become possible when, as we say later in chapters 9, 10 and 11, systematic research, recorded practice and teaching experience provides the necessary further knowledge. In the meantime, it is hoped that some community workers at any level will take advanced university courses in social planning, social administration, sociology and social research method.

An organisational pattern for professional training in community work
It might be helpful at this stage to illustrate a possible pattern for the organisation of professional training for community work (i.e. for the inclusion of community work courses within existing provision leading to the same general qualifications). It is illustrative since the possibilities are within the framework of existing social work courses but a similar pattern might be constructed with reference to courses for administrators or teachers. Our proposal for a one-year course for candidates with certain qualifications (see p. 91) could be fitted into a general pattern.

University or C.N.A.A. degree courses
1. A four-year 'integrated' degree course of two years social studies and two years professional studies.

University courses

2. A degree or diploma in social studies, followed by a one (or sometimes two) year applied social studies course.

3. A degree in any other subject, followed in the main by a university two year applied social studies course.

Other integrated courses of social and professional studies (these are provided at present in university extra-mural departments and colleges of further education)

4. A two (or three) year integrated course of social and professional studies.

The qualifying award

If community work becomes a separate or expanded course within the established pattern, students should receive whatever is the award given at the end of the course, for instance, a degree or diploma in applied social studies. The same principle would apply to courses in colleges of education. This seems to us very much preferable to a separate qualification in community work. We realise there would be difficulties about courses run in colleges of further or higher education (other than for C.N.A.A. degrees) but we hope that these could be overcome by some comprehensive award-granting national council. We refer to this in chapter 12, pp. 146–7.

Selection

Growing interest in broad questions of community action is sufficient to justify optimism about recruitment to well planned professional training for community work, provided that it results in a transferable qualification, with some additional training, that there is a reasonable career structure and that supply does not exceed demand.

Nonetheless, selection will not be easy because little is known about the kind of people who make good community workers, nor, as we have said on p. 92, whether the same people are likely to be equally effective in all three aspects of community work. One of our informants suggested that the most important personal quality necessary in the worker is 'to see the potentialities of a great variety of individuals and groups in relation to local needs and opportunities'.[1] To this may be added potentiality for work which carries a fair degree of independence and initiative, capacities for constructive criticism and for careful observation and analysis of situations which others may take for granted, sensitivity to others and sufficient integrity not to misuse power and influence in situations where the opportunity to manipulate others may be considerable. Many of those, whether men or women, who wish to work at the inter-

1. Communication to the Study Group from Mr Robin Guthrie, Warden of Cambridge House Settlement, Camberwell, 1967.

agency and community planning level are likely to be older, mature candidates.

Existing selection procedures in the courses discussed on pp. 90–4 will no doubt be followed, including associating field teachers with interviewing and decisions. It is essential that careful records should be kept of every candidate at each stage of selection and during and after the course. The analysis of such records, and study of good and bad practice, is the only objective way to learn about necessary qualifications and capacities and what to look for in selection.

Teaching staff
The most difficult problem in considering professional training for community work is not to see how it might fit into existing patterns but how to develop the resources in classroom and field teaching necessary to bring it up to the standard achieved by other professional courses.

Those needed to teach in a community work course are: the lecturers in background subjects, including human growth and behaviour, sociology and social psychology, the social services and social policy (from the angles of administration, applied economics, social history and philosophy) and other less essential or optional subjects; and those who will teach the principles and practice of community work.

It is important that those who are responsible for teaching background and professional subjects respectively should meet periodically as a group to discuss the objectives of the course, the most relevant aspects of each subject and how they are all to be inter-related with each other and with the fieldwork so that students get a good grasp of essentials and are enabled to relate theory to practice. There should always be a senior community work tutor in charge of the course for this and other purposes. The field teachers should be regarded as part of the team.

There are very few people teaching community work here at present and, as we say in chapters 9 and 10, there is little practice theory related to this country, although considerable literature exists about experience elsewhere. A major and time-consuming task thus lies ahead in collecting material about the processes in community work practice, relating this to social science concepts, building up principles of practice from British and other experience, and collecting case records in this country for teaching purposes. Some material will no doubt come from systematic discussions with practitioners, and from working with field teachers. This is also a valuable form of in-service training. It is to be hoped that the staffs of the various community work courses will share case records and other teaching material and also pool experience of using these. It is also desirable that both educational institutions and the national council which we propose (see chapter 12, p. 146) should make available the additional resources necessary for the time-consuming and skilled task of recording, collecting and editing case records and other teaching material.

To raise this teaching to an acceptable level will be a demanding enterprise. There are various ways of doing this in addition to what has been said above. In one instance the prospective tutor to a proposed professional course went to the U.S.A. for a year and subsequently a Fulbright senior fellow came to this country to work with him for a further year on gathering material, starting a project and running in-service training courses, all as preliminaries to starting a professional course.

In another instance, a senior research fellow in community organisation has been appointed to study local social needs and resources and to develop teaching in community organisation. So far this has involved building up local contacts, compiling and collating information, especially about pressing social needs, starting regular fortnightly discussion groups and making preliminary plans for courses for voluntary workers. It has also included three months' study in the United States. An optional course in community organisation has been started for post-graduate social work students and it is hoped in time to develop a fieldwork centre.

Whatever plan is followed, it will be essential for community work teachers to be appointed some time before a new course is actually to start, in order to undertake the necessary study and consultation and also to learn how to plan a curriculum and how to teach. It is to be hoped that the teachers in new and existing courses will share with each other in planning and pooling experience. No doubt some community work teachers will take the six months' course in education for social work at the National Institute for Social Work Training, which includes curriculum planning, working with field teachers, selection of course content, use of research findings, and periods of teaching practice.

When a community work course is started within existing patterns of applied social studies or other courses a good deal will already be known about desirable content and methods. In particular, those who already teach background subjects in these courses will be to some extent aware of what is needed.

All that has been said above about 'training the trainers' also applies to those who plan and teach in in-service training courses. Indeed it is a much more formidable task to produce sufficient community work teachers for these courses than the small number required in the first instance for full time courses. It is very much to be hoped that there will be systematic study of the desirable length, content and educational methods of in-service training courses for different participants in the light of stated objectives.

There is an increasing amount of social research not only in university social study departments but also in polytechnics and to a limited extent in colleges of further education. This is important from the point of view of community work students, many of whom will need some research tools in their work. There is also a small but welcome increase in the number of students studying for higher degrees in sociology and social administration.[1]

The main contribution of the social study departments to professional education is made at present through the courses in casework (applied social studies and mental health) offered by all but a handful of universities. These courses embody the elements found in all training for professional practice and therefore essential in community work. These are the acquisition of knowledge, the ability to see how it applies in particular situations, the development of specific practice skills and appropriate professional attitudes. Professional courses are notoriously overloaded but it is essential to ensure that the demands of the curriculum do not so exceed the students' absorption capacities that they learn to play safe rather than to think.

COURSES FOR MEMBERS OF RELATED PROFESSIONS WITH A COMMUNITY WORK FUNCTION

Three obvious examples of those whose community function is secondary to another primary function are caseworkers, whether in the child care, health and welfare or probation and after-care services; youth leaders and organisers; and some teachers. In the last group those who become teacher/wardens or teacher/youth leaders are at the frontier where informal education and community work are closely interwoven. This also applies to other teachers, particularly in schools which are conscious of their role in the community, in educational priority areas, and to most head teachers: and also increasingly to many working in various branches of further education, all of whom have a substantial community component in their work. All these varied people need a realistic understanding of local communities and why it is important to work with rather than for them.

It is significant that, as we have shown in chapter 5, teaching about group process and community studies and some fieldwork with groups and communities is beginning to be incorporated in casework courses; while students are offered options in youth leadership in some forty colleges of education and in a number of syllabuses there is a fairly substantial community development section.

1. A student at York University is taking an M.Phil. in community organisation and there is a community development option in an M.Sc. course at the London School of Economics, while the M.Ed. in community development can be taken by dissertation at Manchester University.

It is especially desirable for teachers to take a course in community work at the point where they are being promoted to posts where this becomes a significant part of their function. The wish of groups of parents to make better provision for children in the neighbourhood is one of the most potent motives in local community efforts, thus head teachers are in a key position where they can either help forward or ignore local community endeavours. In educational priority areas the schools have a crucial role to play in revitalising deprived neighbourhoods. We hope that university social study departments, institutes and colleges of education, extra-mural departments and polytechnics will all combine to work out the contributions of the social sciences, social work and informal education to community work by teachers and others. Among these others are housing managers and many administrative officers in local government. For this varied group we hope joint in-service training courses of various kinds will be provided.

It is desirable that some – or more – study of the human sciences and their application in understanding local community life should be included in the initial training of architects, doctors,[1] teachers and others. It should also be carried further, preferably through post-graduate study, by those who later have community responsibilities in their work.

At a number of points in this report we have spoken of the importance of community studies in the work of certain senior and chief officers of local authorities, for town planners, architects, and indeed some civil servants. In essence, this entails study of social institutions, social relations and social values in relation to planned (or unplanned) social change (including population changes) in any given segment of local or national affairs.

Every doctor wishing to become a medical officer of health must take a year's course for the diploma in public health, following a syllabus laid down by the General Medical Council, which allows for flexibility within certain prescribed subjects, combined with substantial observation in a health department. This is the only example of a required further qualification for a chief officer in local government. Whether or not further qualifications should be required, it is desirable that those becoming senior or chief officers of local authorities or in certain regional authorities, or inspectors or advisers in certain government departments should undergo relevant study of the human sciences, including social research findings and methods, and the application of community planning techniques which include local community participation. We have mentioned in chapter 5 the hopeful beginnings made at the Institute of Local Government Studies.

1. See the *Report of the Royal Commission on Medical Education*, pp. 104–9 and appendices 10 and 11, pp. 278–80.

Community studies in training or further training for other professions would no doubt take various forms, including substantial post-graduate courses. One of the most valuable of these forms might be refresher courses and conferences in which members of several professions looked at different aspects of community life from the vantage point of their own particular profession and its relations with other professions for the purpose of trying to clarify the inter-related contribution of each social service to the progressive improvement of living conditions in the locality. The staff college type of syndicate, combined with field projects, would be appropriate educational devices for this purpose.

This completes what we have to say in brief about the general pattern of training for full time professional community workers, as well as for members of other professions, part of whose function is in direct work with local communities or else entails decisions about needs, priorities and planning that intimately affects the quality of life for local communities.

IN-SERVICE TRAINING

In any comprehensive strategy for training it is essential to provide both full time professional courses and a varied range of in-service training. By in-service training is meant opportunities for staff already in post to take courses of various kinds. These would include a range of introductory and refresher courses as well as secondment to take a full time course or for further study or advanced training: the days are past when the original professional qualification was assumed to be 'an act of salvation after which one is safe for eternity'.[1] This principle is well established in medicine, teaching and social work. Those who should have planned opportunities for further learning are not only the trained, who need the chance as time goes on to consolidate and expand their knowledge and skill, but also the untrained, whether experienced people or new recruits, who are likely to be employed in community work for some time to come.

Community workers are particularly vulnerable to social change, indeed sensitivity to change and its impact on people's lives is at the heart of their work. This means that all community workers should have continuing opportunities for in-service training at appropriate intervals in their career, whether provided by their employing authority, educational institutions or professional associations. Some courses might be general, others focused on some particular aspect, for example, work with tenants on new housing estates, in deprived areas, with immigrants, or with young people. Others yet might be on the sociological study of an area, or social research techniques,

1. Sir Eric Ashby, in an address to the British Association, August 1963.

or working with groups on priority planning, or inter-agency cooperation, or on forecasting changing social needs. It is most desirable that some courses should be jointly run for community workers and members of other professions. We have referred already to the need for substantial post-graduate studies for those taking on wider administrative or consultative responsibilities.

So far as length is concerned, in-service training usually consists of two- or three-day full time courses; of day release courses spread over a longer period; of five- or ten-day conferences, or various other lengths and combinations of time. A useful educational pattern is a short full time period, followed by a return to work with an assignment and follow up, and then another full time period. All these patterns have their merits, though no one knows exactly what these are. Much more recording, comparative study and evaluation are necessary to discover what time periods provide the best learning experience, what intervals reinforce learning and lead to a new level for the next study period.

It is desirable that all newly appointed workers (whether qualified or not) should have an induction course and a period of field teaching in their employing agency.

Each piece of in-service training should come at the participant's maximum point of need and receptivity. This will also affect the content and educational method to be used. For example, newly qualified students seem to benefit in the first year after training from two return periods appropriately spaced (no one knows exactly what this may be) to the college where they qualified. In the first period time must be allocated for group discussions with opportunities to express grouses, anxieties and the struggle to apply in real work situations what the students learned on the course. The second period comes after the sometimes depressive adjustment stage and helps to consolidate learning and carry it further. The feeling of the group for its members is particularly important in these as in other courses.

One of the aims of in-service training should be to give participants as much experience as possible of the improved application of methods which they themselves are using in their work. It should never take the form of one group 'teaching' or 'telling' another. There is considerable knowledge and wisdom amongst participants taking an in-service training course and the aim should be to draw this out, to enable them to know what they know, to systematise it and carry it further so that they are better equipped to go on learning.

Although it is valuable to go away from the job from time to time for in-service training, this is not a substitute for real on-the-job learning. People must be enabled to go on learning creatively from their own experience. This requires regular opportunities for group discussion, pooling of experience and recording of successful or unsuccessful activity under the guidance of more experienced community workers with teaching experience.

It is the responsibility of employing authorities to promote in-service training and to second community workers to suitable courses. Provision of in-service training is both facilitated and made more efficient if it is the responsibility of a senior official in the agency. No doubt the Local Government Training Board will make an important contribution in this field, as to other aspects of training. The actual provision of in-service training courses may be within the employing authority or at universities or colleges of further education or arranged by professional associations or voluntary organisations. Voluntary organisations should be given financial and other help for in-service training and secondment.

If staff development is an obligation of employing agencies, and professional people have a duty to go on learning, then educational institutions also have a duty to provide suitable opportunities for this. In so doing their teaching staff will have much to gain from discussion with senior experienced people with wide knowledge of the realities of community work.

EVALUATION

The new courses in community work, whether professional or in-service training, will provide an important opportunity for built-in evaluation from the start, making explicit the assumptions on which they are planned, the methods and aims of student selection, the objectives of the courses in relation to curriculum planning, educational method and the means of assessing students. We hope all this will be systematically recorded as part of a research project and that students will be followed up at stated intervals for at least their first three years in employment to test what they are using of what they have learned or what has been lacking.

It is also desirable that teachers of community work (including field teachers) should get together regularly to pool experience on student selection, the theoretical and practical content of the courses, educational method, and student assessment.

9

The Contribution of the Social Sciences and Other Subjects

A BASIS FOR SELECTION

To supplement and challenge our own ideas about the contribution which the social sciences, particularly sociology and psychology, can make to an understanding of community processes and to the training of community workers, we consulted a number of university teachers in several disciplines in Britain and from the U.S.A. (see appendix A). Their contribution provides much of the material for this chapter.

It helped to shed light on a basis for relevant selection within the vast range of the social sciences, divided as they are between a number of disciplines each with material for a lifetime study. It must be remembered that community work training does not require students to become experts in the individual social sciences. The central issue, therefore, is to determine the basis for selection.[1] In community work, as in other spheres where given sciences are used to underpin practice, this necessitates clarity about the central task – what configuration of activities and purpose distinguishes any particular practice from others. We have already said in chapters 4 (p. 42) and 6 (p. 67) that in community work the two main functions are first analysis of a given social situation, and second the ability to make and use relationships with individuals and groups in order to carry forward and influence the course of social change. For its accomplishment this requires relevant knowledge from the social sciences, the disciplined use of skill in application, and ethical constraints on the use of the community worker's influence.

PROBLEMS OF SELECTING MATERIAL FROM THE SOCIAL SCIENCES

The concept of training provides a useful basis for selection within the social sciences. Unlike the term education, training assumes an activity for which students are being prepared and by implication that there are certain areas of knowledge of special relevance to practice. Training, moreover, is not just an intellectual activity, but, as has been said above, includes the acquisition of knowledge, skills and professional attitudes. This applies no matter what type, level or length of training is under consideration. Therefore we have

1. For a more detailed and general discussion see *The Contribution of Social Sciences in Social Work Training*, Unesco, Paris, 1960.

chosen a framework for social science study related to training rather than to purely educational needs.

If criteria on the lines of those outlined above are used in the selection and combination of material from the social sciences, this means that community work teachers must take an active part in this rather than expecting the social sciences to produce some magic 'integrated theory'. Inevitably selection must be based upon the specific roles of community workers and be developed into a coherent systematic body of knowledge which distinguishes community work from other functions. Neither psychology nor sociology can supply this integration, nor should they be expected to do so. Community work training must therefore be based on a selection from the social sciences in the light of what the community worker really needs to know for his own purposes, not for those of the social scientist.[1] This is a demanding task on which some work has been done already but much remains to be done as training in both theory and practice is more systematically developed.

THE IMPORTANCE OF DEVELOPING A THEORY OF PRACTICE

Our interest in the social sciences stems from concern that community work largely lacks a conceptual framework or systematic evidence about the effectiveness of its methods. In the meantime, many community workers are already active in different fields and this number is likely to grow. Further knowledge could be gained by a systematic analysis in the light of relevant social science concepts of the tasks and working methods of existing community workers, whether full time or using this approach for another professional task or as voluntary workers. In addition, organisational analysis might help to show what kind of administrative structures are needed to meet multiple rather than single needs, say those of a racially mixed population rather than the needs of a specific clientele within it, and how organisational constraints affect practice. Evidence from the everyday practice of community work, based on systematic collection of data and the formulation of testable hypotheses derived from experience is necessary if we are to build up a theory of practice. An analysis of community tasks and the administrative settings and constraints within which they are attempted is a necessary element in discovering how to select knowledge from the social sciences and apply it to the practice of community work. This exercise would no doubt lead to redefining a number of tasks and give greater precision to viable means of achieving realistic objectives. It would also clarify some of the many points at which further social research is needed.

It is desirable that in systematic reporting by community workers of

1. The foregoing is based on a communication to the Study Group from Dr George Thomason, University College, Cardiff, 1968.

their actual tasks, they should have at their disposal the kind of background social science and other knowledge discussed later in this chapter. In any event, practitioners, community work teachers and others must embark upon the continuing task of relating actual practice and relevant social science knowledge to each other. Much of this will depend on and grow from training. In social group work and in casework research and practice have begun to reinforce each other, and this experience should have something to contribute to community work. The actual content of a possible course on principles and practice of community work at the present time is outlined in the specimen syllabus in appendix D.

A FRAMEWORK FOR CURRICULUM PLANNING

If the syllabus should be built around the demands of the job within the general framework of social situation analysis and group relationships for the purpose of bringing about some social change, what are the significant considerations for curriculum planning?

First there is the worker himself as a person who needs a certain educational background and personal qualities and who must be helped to develop more self-awareness about his feelings, prejudices and values. He must become more skilled at making and using relationships, more aware of his strengths and weaknesses in different aspects of his work.

Second, there are methods of work and the tools of his trade:

(a) What is entailed in study of the 'community', the kind of social situation analysis referred to in chapters 4 and 5? What are the sources of information and the alternative methods for gathering data and interpreting it?

(b) How does the worker set about administrative tasks, e.g. in developing programmes, in working with his own and other agencies, in recording and in reporting?

Third, there are some of the skills:

(a) How does the worker involve himself with key groups and with key persons in his job? How does he foster and use good working relationships with local people? What is implied in the nature of his relationships with leaders, with conflicting groups? What are his professional responsibilities and loyalties *vis-à-vis* a bureaucratic structure?

(b) What skills in human relations does he need, particularly in working with groups? What enabling, facilitating, educational, public relations, administrative and other skills does he need?

These questions lead to a further issue of how the necessary knowledge, skill and attitudes can be most effectively acquired within the time limits of a particular course and given the students' background and abilities. Obviously the answer to this lies in well-planned field-work as well as background and professional studies. This chapter concentrates on the background subjects, chapter 10 on educational method and the principles and practice of community work and chapter 11 on the parallel fieldwork.

THE CONTRIBUTION OF THE SOCIAL SCIENCES

The following are some basic questions to be asked in relation to the social sciences:

1. What can they tell us about the nature of 'community' in con-temporary society? What kinds of 'community' are there? What are the conflicts inherent in them and between them? What is the nature and process of social change and resistances to change within the different elements of the social structure? In short, how far has there been a conceptualisation of 'community' processes which might provide one part of a theory relevant to community work? In practice the reality of 'community' and community work lies not in abstract terms, but in particular tasks in voluntary organisations or statutory authorities. These may arise from the frustrations of families in large blocks of flats, or the tensions between immigrants and an existing population in a town, or the lack of cooperation and coordinated planning between social agencies, or the more general social needs which arise in a new town, or grow amongst the residents in a suburb. Social science can throw a good deal of light on particular problems thus defined.

2. What are the tasks and limitations imposed by agency practice or by other social forces upon community work of different kinds? What kinds of professional persons are needed to fulfil these tasks? Assuming there are different 'communities' and within these some potentiality for change, what are the processes and the conse-quences of conscious intervention by community workers to promote change or maintain stability? What is the evidence supporting community work as such, at different levels and with different approaches?

3. How could social science findings be related to the tasks and methodology of community work to provide effective training? What are the limitations of knowledge in the social sciences in this respect? What balance should be struck between the several social science disciplines and what common ground exists?

4. Are there distinct areas of knowledge appropriate to each type of community work or is it legitimate to accept a generic base? On reflection both the Study Group and the social scientists

emphasised the common elements in the knowledge needed by all types of community worker.

It seems clear that psychology, sociology and political, administrative and economic studies should all contribute to training, as well as at least elementary research methods and skills and methods for evaluating the worker's interventions, together with the administrative, legal and other constraints or aids which condition community work activities.

It is significant that in expressing views about some of the issues we raised, the social scientists emphasised that how to present a subject is as important as what to teach.[1] Some methods of applied social science will be useful in classroom and fieldwork teaching, for example, experimental groups, project analysis, interviewing and recording. What follows is largely based on the views of the social scientists whom we consulted.

The contribution of psychology

From psychology should come deeper understanding of the individual, including both the worker himself and those with whom he works. The interrelationship between individuals and the various groups in which they interact is complex and not well understood, but clearly of vital importance to the community worker. This study will include an understanding of the dynamics of human behaviour, of the ways in which what people feel determines their behaviour, how their life experience can affect current attitudes, the relations between feelings of security and self-confidence – or the lack of these – and ability to take part in community affairs, and ways in which small group membership can be used to increase capacity for social relationships.

H. M. Holden suggested that:

All workers should have a thorough grounding in the understanding of human relations and, even more important, this training should include supervised 'grass roots' work with individuals and their families. I would hope the basic course would include a series of lecture discussions on human growth and development considered within the framework of the family and the social group.

He added:

It must be recognised that the experience of working closely with socially deprived and often very disturbed individuals or groups is

1. We regret that because of lack of space we have not been able to include detailed syllabuses sent by Mrs M. Stacey, University College, Swansea, and Professor Elliott Jaques, Brunel University, 1967.

enormously threatening, especially to students and newly appointed workers, since it tends to bring out their own latent conflicts and disturbances. In my view some support structure for community workers is essential.[1]

G. M. Carstairs wrote:

The contribution of social psychiatry to the training you are suggesting would be both theoretical and practical. We could share in the teaching about personality development, stressing the influence of group experience. We could discuss the acquisition of attitudes and value systems. We could also give an account of the commoner forms of psychopathology, stressing neurosis and personality disorder. . . . Practical instruction would consist in letting students observe the range of activities in community psychiatry. . . . Part of this experience should be sufficiently prolonged to allow students to participate as members of the therapeutic team.[2]

Elliott Jaques emphasised the importance of psychology in analysing interpersonal behaviour and suggested that the syllabus should cover topics such as social perception, social learning, attitude formation and change.[3] In addition both he and D. E. G. Plowman[4] stressed the contribution of psychology to the study of groups, of forms of communication and of professionalisation.

The study of psychology should include the following:

1. The processes of physical and psychological growth and functioning through the life-span.
2. Interrelationships between physical, psychological and social factors.
3. The family. Personality patterns and deviation.
4. Social perception, interpersonal stimulus and response, social learning, attitude formation, stereotyping and prejudice, attitude change, including an introduction to the structure and function of language in interpersonal communication.
5. Human groups. Group structure and function; experimental investigation of group behaviour; use of groups in teaching, learning and therapy; individuals in relation to groups and institutions and groups in relation to institutions; leadership.

1. Communication from Dr H. M. Holden, Tavistock Institute of Human Relations, London, 1967.
2. Communication from Professor G. M. Carstairs, University of Edinburgh, 1967.
3. Communication from Professor Elliott Jacques, Brunel University, 1967.
4. Communication from Mr D. E. G. Plowman, London School of Economics, 1967.

Another set of helpful suggestions about social psychology came from discussions with Professor Marie Jahoda of the University of Sussex. She proposed concentration on a number of basic concepts in the behavioural sciences, taught not didactically but as far as possible through the experience of the students. The concepts could be illustrated by a study of points in life cycles, based on case studies of individuals and families from different parts of society. These could then be interpreted within changing social structures over time, and contrasts made between the differing experiences of individuals and of social groups within different occupational and cultural settings. Professor Jahoda's key concepts were: culture (values and norms), role, status, social class, social groups, and personality. The middle level type of theory, such as that of R. K. Merton,[1] seemed to her the most appropriate and the teaching might most usefully combine seminars which identified student interest and knowledge, and quite stiff and rigorous lectures on academic and conceptual material, with intervening discussion to relate theory and practice.

She also suggested that the close parallels between the main steps in the research process and the steps taken in practice by the community worker should be brought out in teaching. The research worker defines his problem, forms a hypothesis, collects relevant data, reviews his hypothesis and reinterprets his data. Similarly, the community worker starts with a problem, collects evidence, attempts a diagnosis, makes an assessment to decide what he can do about the problem, and in the course of action is constantly rethinking both his assessment and his method. The assumption here is that a practical situation presents, as it were, a research problem and the systematic research approach can perhaps usefully be taught as part of a course on methods.

The contribution of sociology

Sociology offers a major and valuable contribution to a community work course. In terms of interdisciplinary study, sociology shares with anthropology and social psychology common territory and common methods of study, while some concepts of the three disciplines overlap. Sociology also has interests in administrative and political questions and notably in problems of organisation. Industrial sociology is also significant. One member of the Study Group, Dr D. F. Swift, has produced an extensive list of readings in community organisation and development, based largely on sociological literature,[2] and we also had a good deal of material from the U.S.A.

1. R. K. Merton, *Social Theory and Social Structure*, Free Press, Glencoe, 1957, esp. pp. 50–6.
2. 'Readings in community organisation and development in a modern industrial society', ed. D. F. Swift, Department of Education, University of Oxford, unpublished typescript.

Mrs Stacey suggested the following frames for selecting sociological materials:

1. A knowledge of how society works now, especially the inter-relations of institutions within the society, including the value and beliefs systems of the society and its parts.
2. The meanings in terms of social position for individuals and for groups of the prevailing social structure and culture.
3. A knowledge of what changes are taking place (*a*) internally within the society under study, and (*b*) externally to it but bearing upon it and inducing changes in it.
4. In purposefully induced change, and given the direction in which it has been decided that change is wanted, sociology should aid towards an understanding of (*a*) the constraints which will impede such change and the forces which will be on its side; (*b*) the values underlying the change and how they are consonant or dissonant with the existing values of the individuals, groups and systems in the society.
5. Formal and large-scale organisations; an examination of the structure of such large-scale organisations as works, schools, local authorities, and of the roles, statuses, the norms and values, goals and type of social relations involved, viewed from the position of an employee and a client or customer. A major component would be the study of communication and the management of innovation.[1]

The following could well be added to Mrs Stacey's suggestions: the nature of professionalism; the impact of values on professional knowledge and activity; the employment and use of professionals in bureaucratic settings; and relevant aspects of role theory as a means of understanding how individuals are related to social systems; the nature of role relationships; what is implied in the increasing complexity of such relationships; role demands; role conflict; and relations between role, cultural values and social change.

Mrs Stacey went on to say:

While it is true that one can and should analytically distinguish between sociology and social philosophy it is possible that in practice there is no sociologist whose work, either at the level of theory or empirical activity, is unaffected by his own ethical decisions. The same is obviously true of the social worker. This phenomenon can, and to my mind should, itself be studied by sociologists. Thus the community worker has need to understand his own social position and its related values. This is the sociological equivalent of a

1. Communication from Mrs Margaret Stacey.

psychological understanding of oneself which has long been recognised as essential for social workers.*

In any applied course which is specifically designed to serve vocational ends, in some way, the orientation of the course is as important as its subject matter, so that the content and approach may not only be relevant but be seen to be relevant. In principle, therefore, a wise approach is to start from the situation in which the worker finds himself, or in which he can be expected to find himself in the vocation for which he is training. Applied courses should to my mind be built outwards from the sociological aspects of this situation rather than follow the neat pattern of academic logic.

In conclusion, it seems to me that, at whatever level of community involvement a worker finds himself, the same general sociological knowledge would be helpful to him. The principal differences that one might propose in courses . . . would be in (a) their starting point and (b) the weight given to the various parts of the course, rather than in the overall content of the course.

Paul Stirling, trained in social anthropology but currently a Professor of Sociology, wrote:

As social animals, reacting to other people within a social organisation, we have culturally given built-in 'models' both of what is going on around us, and of what ought to be going on around us. Sociology implies temporarily at least suspending both these factual assumptions and these values to see if they are plausible and sensible. For most people this is a difficult and uncomfortable exercise. Hence teaching people to think sociologically often takes quite a time, even if the course is intensive. If the course is too much concerned with concepts and generalities, the students fail to see its implications and its relevance to their own situation; if it is too factual and ethnographic, they reinterpret the data in their own values and categories and miss the point.

The method of teaching I would advocate therefore is to begin the course with specific descriptive studies of 'communities'. Since really closed subsistence societies no longer exist in the United Kingdom, I would strongly recommend including one or two village studies in other cultures, as well as one or two from our own; the teacher should raise the theoretical problems about roles, sanctions, networks, so that the theoretical insights arise from actual data. For example, the distinction between 'many-stranded' relationships and 'single-stranded' relationships seems to me one of fundamental significance, which can best be grasped

* Lewis Coser's analysis of Georg Simmel's social position and its consequences for Simmel's activities is an example of this point from the academic field. *Georg Simmel*, ed. Lewis A. Coser, Prentice Hall, 1965, pp. 29–42.

by a study of relatively closed societies where many-stranded relationships abound. Only with the growth of large-scale urban-based societies have single-stranded relationships become a part of the experience of people in general rather than of a small elite. Allied to this problem is the more complex one of typology of 'associations' distinguishing 'single purpose' associations from 'multi-functional' associations.

The introduction of some non-European studies (e.g. caste villages) has another advantage. People are more likely to be able to examine their own values objectively if they have succeeded in suspending moral judgements on people of a different culture.[1]

While there is considerable literature on the nature of community both in Britain and the U.S.A., and even more from anthropological studies of traditional societies, nowhere does this lead to any agreed conceptualisation of what is meant by the term community in complex, mobile, industrial societies, nor what are the many different social systems, processes of change and of conflict within such societies. Clearly there are many types of 'community' and many processes of social change. A comprehensive theory of community may not be possible since the structure of social relationships is both complex and variable. Several of the social scientists drew attention to the danger of definitions which confuse moral or romantic ideas about community life for which there is little objective evidence.

Gerald Popplestone discussed the question as follows:

Community development workers generally assume that people live in localities that are (or can become) 'communities' or areas that provide situations through which the inhabitants can form mutualities that provide outlet for individual or group needs. However, the lack of an adequate conceptual framework relating 'individual' and 'community', which takes account of the influence of social structure on an individual's behaviour and of the relationship between different types of technological development and the ensuing social structure, makes it easy for the assumptions about community life to be inappropriate to particular situations. Indeed, the models of the 'ideal' communities that the field worker may have, are often based on models that rarely exist in modern, industrialised Britain.[2]

Paul Stirling wrote:

It can be misleading to talk of 'breakdown' of communities. Any set of people living in a 'locality', even in preliterate societies, will have some relationships that lead outside the locality. At one

1. Communication from Professor Paul Stirling, University of Kent, 1967.
2. Communication from Mr G. Popplestone, University of Aberdeen, 1967.

extreme, a subsistence agricultural area may have relatively few, largely confined to headmen or the village leaders. Even these outgoing relationships are fundamental in the lives of all the people since they are always of great economic and political importance, involving the acceptance of orders from outside, and the exchange of some products for imports into the village; moreover, they imply a wealthy important class not tied as they are to a 'community'. At the other extreme, a modern suburban housing estate may consist of people with intense social networks, who yet have almost nothing to do with each other at all. Between these 'polar types' are a vast variety of types of 'social structure' in different localities. In all of them, in general, the higher a person's social rank, the less local his social relationships. And the more advanced the society, the less, relatively, the importance of relationships within the locality. Most change is therefore away from what some people think of as 'community' but it does not follow that anything at all has broken down.

Later he commented:

[We can] seriously understate the case for accepting conflict as part of human existence. All villages, all professions, all workshops are full of struggles for power and prestige, disputes on land, jobs, pay, privilege, resentment of authority and so forth. If some are in office others must be excluded. Problems of legitimation and compliance apply to community organisations as to any others. Indeed, any successful cooperation at any point in a social structure necessarily implies conflict and tension at some other.

These comments suggest some of the inherent difficulties in defining community in any of the traditional senses of close neighbourliness or even multiple interaction between groups of people within a locality. They suggest the importance of some element of deprivation, of conflict, or of absence of close social ties, as practical elements in creating a need for community work.

It is clear that sociology and social psychology are likely to provide not only much of the basic theory about community work but also important factual knowledge about social structure, social system analysis and quantified facts on social change. Indeed theoretical study of difficult and disputed concepts such as community, community process, social change, alienation and conflict is useful in clarifying actual situations and tasks.

As Roger Wilson puts it:

The factors that have a bearing on how people live among their neighbours and the relationships between them are both sociological and psychological: stresses and strains . . . are internal things which may or may not produce external symptoms. . . . [They] happen *inside* people and, if we want to understand what they are and what they mean to their possessors and how the outward signs of them affect their neighbours, we have to look both at the external sociological features which envelop everybody and at the psychological factors of individual persons and their families, which determine how they interpret these features to themselves and how they feel about them.[1]

The contribution of economics and social history

Some aspects of economics and of social history are highly relevant. Community workers must make systematic study of the economic and historical aspects of social policy and of family and community life in the context of social change. Economic studies are clearly necessary when community workers are largely concerned with priorities in the allocation of resources and the relation between social and economic elements in planning.

Methods of social investigation

To these basic contributions from the social sciences must be added the study of at least elementary methods of social investigation comprising an understanding of social research methods, elementary statistics and computer uses. The community worker has to be able to collaborate effectively with social researchers, to understand, assess and utilise a variety of research findings and to undertake certain forms of investigation himself. More generally, an understanding of research methods can foster the objectivity in observation and analysis to which reference has already been made, while the stages of the research process itself parallel those involved in community work.

The contribution of politics, government and social administration

Since the professional community worker is employed within an administrative structure and much of his work involves administrative relationships, up and down and across, he needs both factual and analytical knowledge of social administration and political science. First, there is what might be broadly termed government and politics, including a consideration of central and local government, public administration and political science; second, the study of the social services and social policy or social administration, that is of social problems and society's response to them by statutory provision and voluntary action.

T. E. Chester put it this way:

1. Wilson, *Difficult Housing Estates*, p. 8.

Social administration would be highly relevant. . . . For example, the face-to-face level worker would require considerable knowledge of social problems to facilitate his understanding of the neighbourhood in which he works. Without a wide knowledge of, for example, things like the prevalence of poverty, the housing shortage, child deprivation, etc., he would be unable to assess the problems of his particular neighbourhood with any realism or sense of proportion. Similarly, in his object of helping the inhabitants to achieve their goals, he would need considerable knowledge of the social services, which is fundamental to any form of social work, including community work. The second type of worker, the inter-agency coordinator, operating in the local authorities setting would obviously need quite a detailed knowledge of social provision and social policy in order to be effective. His study would have to be analytical and critical rather than merely factually descriptive. For example, it would need to provide a lively awareness of a dynamic nature of social needs and provision, together with a grasp of the organisational and administrative difficulties militating against optimum flexibility in social services.[1]

Professor Elliott Jaques wrote:

It is imperative that [a course in social administration] should be a real analysis of administration and administrative institutions, and not just a set of descriptions, so that it demands from students a continuous assessment of the structure of personal and social welfare organisations and their aptness for the functions they are required to perform. This is not, however, to undervalue a firm grasp of factual detail, for this particular worker must be equipped to enable the community and its members to utilise existing resources, in view of the difficulties of enlarging these radically in the near future.

There are clearly difficulties in balancing content between what is descriptive and factual and what is conceptual. While not underestimating the importance of strictly factual information, the more searching and analytical material is likely to be of greater use, based as it should be on empirical studies. The range of such studies as organisation theory, administrative behaviour, power and conflict, to mention but a few, lead into questions on decision making, communication, formal and informal social structure, innovation, leadership and much else of immediate relevance to community work. There is the added advantage that these studies have close links with sociology, with social psychology and applied economics.

1. Communication from Professor T. E. Chester, University of Manchester, 1967.

They thus help to give a syllabus cohesion by focusing several disciplines upon a particular area of community work.

THE IMPORTANCE OF SOCIAL PHILOSOPHY

Cutting into the need to establish a relevant social sciences frame of reference is the fact that community workers can never rely on the social sciences only for background knowledge. Their tasks in intervening in the human situation, their interest in social change, their concern with social dysfunction, as they or their agencies see it, mean that social philosophy becomes another important frame of reference. The objectives, the methods, the results of community work are as much determined by beliefs and values as they are by social science. Indeed many would realistically argue that certain social sciences might well provide tools for manipulation and that agreed ethical codes are necessary as a safeguard. Equally, the social scientist would argue that the dangers of community work lie in their untested value assumptions and the risk that unintended consequences of initiated change may mean that the pursuit of one end results in other ethically undesirable consequences.

Mrs Stacey commented on these questions as follows:

It seems to me that two separate social frames of reference are involved: (i) that of sociology and (ii) that of social philosophy. The ethical and philosophical decisions about what is good or bad in society as it stands cannot be decided by sociologists. Nor can sociologists decide whether it is good or bad for an individual or group to alter his/its position in society. Nevertheless, the implications of these ethical and philosophical decisions cannot be ignored in applied sociology.

Community work cannot but be saturated with value judgements and assumptions both in terms of the ends it serves and the means it employs. Examination of values is therefore essential in the teaching of government and politics and of social administration; and above all in the teaching of principles and practice of community work where the focus moves from academic discussion to principles and methods of action.

As Paul Stirling put it:

We need continually to ask what we are trying to change and whether we are quite sure the second state will be better than the first. We also need to ask why the non-joiners do not join, and why the non-askers do not ask when they need help. If we go beyond this point to supposing that we know better than other people what they ought to do with their spare time, or how they

115

ought to arrange their social relationships, we are taking grave risks. It seems to me that sociology has a very important role here in forcing workers and administrators to ask these questions before they act on unquestioned assumptions about the desirability of sponsored as opposed to spontaneous contacts, of getting together as opposed to going to the pictures alone, or visiting friends outside the locality.

The question which remains is whether some direct consideration of values and ethics from a philosophical standpoint would aid the student's learning. In the words of Professor Emmet:

. . . there are considerations by which both sociology and ethics can be justified in their own right and each contains independent arguments for its theories. But . . . they are not so completely independent and autonomous that what goes on in the one has no relevance in the other. There may be some sociological questions which are also in part ethical questions and vice versa. The inference to be drawn, if I am right, is that a sociologist may be a better sociologist by being a reasonably sophisticated moralist, and a moralist may be a better moralist if he can enlarge his vision through a 'general orientation' gained from an interest in sociology. It may even be that the combination of the two interests may contribute something to understanding the situations in which we ask the painful substantive question, 'What ought I to do?'.[1]

AMERICAN EXPERIENCE

While the Study Group was meeting, parallel discussions on the training and functions of community workers were proceeding in the U.S.A., notably through the major project on 'Community Organisation Curriculum Development' under the Council on Social Work Education referred to in chapter 5, pp. 59–60.

A dominant note in the American approach to professional training is the emphasis on the tasks to be tackled and on the roles of the worker in relation to these concrete tasks. They start with practice and move out from there towards theory. In reviewing the existing community organisation courses, the Project progress report comments:

The community organisation courses are conceived primarily as methods courses and it is left to other courses in the curriculum to provide the knowledge that is relevant to the utilisation of the method. For example, many of the issues which will face the community organisation practitioner or the social planners are

1. Dorothy Emmet, *Rules, Roles and Relations*, Macmillan, 1966, p. 5.

covered in courses which carry such labels as 'social policy' and 'social services'. The background of social science theory on which community organisation must rest, is contained in part in community organisation methods courses, but also to a larger extent in courses that deal with the social environment and with group and social processes.[1]

Or again:

> Since there is no integrated social theory that provides systematic unified frameworks for community organisation practice, the theoretical structure will have to be built up from a number of different areas spread over several disciplines.[2]

Professor Bernard Ross of Bryn Mawr College suggested to us that much of the demand for knowledge would grow from the fieldwork and in particular embrace the following:

1. The worker's place in bureaucratic structures.
2. The constant need to be clear about values, e.g. democratic commitment, use of authority, conflicts between goals of the employing agency and the 'community'.
3. The worker's capacity to assess situations.

In examining the tasks which are the professional concern of community organisation students, Professor Martin Rein,[3] also of Bryn Mawr College, emphasised to us that community organisation cannot be considered as a single process. It has many goals with many strategies. There are also many communities and we cannot assume that helping one will help them all. We can consider social participation as one task, possibly as a form of social therapy, leading to both reform and adjustment; coordination as a means of making more effective a wider range of community resources; planning as a means of achieving policy goals. All these raise questions of value judgements which should not be decided on the basis of the findings of social science alone. Robert Perlman wrote:

> There is often a tendency to think of 'the community' as a single entity, but this may obscure important elements and relationships. For example, the concept of 'the people' as constituting the community is not really appropriate to urban, industrialised areas where

1. *Community Organisation Curriculum Development Project, Progress Report*, Council on Social Work Education, New York, 1966, p. 8.

2. *Ibid., Project Plan*, p. 10.

3. See also P. Marris and M. Rein, *Dilemmas of Social Reform: Poverty and Community Action in the United States*, Routledge & Kegan Paul, 1967.

one must also take account of the organisations which serve people.

There is a similar tendency to stress the unity and harmony of the community at the expense of not recognising the equally valid aspects of competition and conflict which stem from difference in needs, functions and values among groups and organisations. Many organisations in fact represent particular interests in a community and much of community work is concerned with, and conditioned by, the processes of competition and accommodation among such groups.

It is also an oversimplification to think of the community only in terms of a small, local geographic area. The growing centralisation of control and decision-making (however much one may deplore it) is a fact which must be taken into account. One must be alert to the limitations of action on a local or neighbourhood basis; such action may fail to change a situation when the sources of control over necessary resources are located far beyond the confines of the local 'community', perhaps in the national government. Certain goals and tasks are certainly appropriate for local community development work; others involving decisions at higher levels will require different forms of social organisation and action. In short, the 'community' is defined differently depending on the context, the goals and the area of action involved.[1]

It is clear that a main concern in the U.S.A. is to develop a viable practice theory, to use the American term. In this, organisation theory, knowledge of public finance and administration, political sociology and study of the methods in community action, play the central roles. It is important to remember, however, that many students entering American schools of social work have had undergraduate courses in the social sciences and that there are, in the syllabus for the master's degree in social work, courses in psychology, sociology and social research for all students (see also chapter 5, p. 60).

CONCLUSIONS

In brief, so far as well selected and coordinated background studies are concerned, we regard sociology and psychology as the two central disciplines, though we are also well aware of the importance of social history and more applied studies in organisation, administration and economics. The social science perspective and the other perspective of social philosophy are both essential. The social sciences can illuminate the cultural elements in value assumptions, provide correctives to untested assumptions and clarify the effect on social

1. Communication from Professor Robert Perlman, Brandeis University, Massachusetts, 1967.

behaviour of value systems, but not what people 'ought' or 'ought not' to believe and do. Also, they may show up some of the intended or unintended consequences of action, but have as yet no certainty in prediction.

From the point of view of curriculum planning, the place of the social sciences in training includes relevant background and applied knowledge and their contribution to the development of practice theory, both in teaching and fieldwork. There is already a good deal to build on. The many unanswered or half-answered questions will, we hope, be further clarified as teachers both of community work and the social sciences discuss together what subject matter students most need to become competent practitioners, and as practice itself is both studied and improved. Community workers, in common with many other professionals, live and work with uncertainty. Greater clarity will only come from the growth of knowledge about human behaviour, from study of practice, from the development of theory related to practice and from continuing research and experimentation.

10

Proposed Content of Training: Theory and Educational Method

CRITERIA FOR PLANNING SPECIFIC COURSES

This chapter discusses the content and methods of training for community work in general terms in order to provide a basis for the planning of specific training activities of all kinds. It takes as its starting-point, therefore, students with little directly relevant background in terms of either education or experience being prepared for a broad range of community work tasks through a substantial period of full time study and experience. The aim of all courses, whether full time or part time, is the development of appropriate attitudes, knowledge and skill in community work. Any particular training activity would involve a realistic selection and modification of the total content in relation to its purpose and resources. More specific selection would also be made in short in-service training courses or in initial or further training courses for caseworkers, teachers, youth leaders, clergy or others.

In order to design and implement appropriate training activities it is essential to take account of the following principles of selection:

1. the purpose of the particular course;
2. its length;
3. the students' background;
4. the roles for which they are being prepared;
5. the resources available.

These in relation with each other determine the content of any specific training. The following discussion of the content and methods of training must be considered throughout with these criteria in mind.

Teaching staff and materials, and satisfactory opportunities for field training, will have to be brought into existence as training expands. They all have repercussions on the objectives, content and methods of training.

TRAINING OBJECTIVES

The experience, knowledge, skills, personal abilities and attitudes with which students come to a course are clearly of major importance in determining reasonable objectives and content, level and pace of training. Some of the desirable content will be beyond the level of some students, at least without lengthy preparation, while for others a good deal of it can be assumed. The previous experience, knowledge and level of performance of the students will affect the desirable length and objectives of training. These objectives will clearly be more comprehensive in a full time qualifying course than in an in-service training course for a specific purpose.

The roles and functions for which students are to be prepared, both immediately on completion of training and in the longer term, should determine the objectives of training. This would in turn have implications for the selection of students and the length of the course. In practice, objectives may need to be modified in relation to the students to be trained and the time available.

Community work covers a very broad range of activity. For particular categories of worker it would be possible to state clear training objectives but even for such workers it would usually not be desirable to focus their training too narrowly. More often training will involve various categories of community worker and objectives will have to be correspondingly broader, although it may be possible to meet the particular requirements of individuals and groups within the total curriculum. In this discussion we are primarily concerned with full time community workers, on the assumption that to clarify the content of their training will provide a basis for deciding what is most essential for others, like teachers, the clergy or caseworkers for whom community work is part of their function.

The knowledge and skills needed by community workers at field, inter-agency or planning levels have been discussed in chapter 6. At the extremes, it would not be realistic to combine within the same course training for what may sometimes be social therapy in a small neighbourhood with large-scale social planning techniques.

It seems likely that the main purpose of full time training at present will be to prepare people for tasks embracing in varying degrees work with community groups and interorganisation and joint planning activities.

METHODS OF TEACHING THE SOCIAL SCIENCES

As we said in the preceding chapter, there is no unified body of social science theory and knowledge which can be made available to students. Professor Roland Warren puts it thus:

> I am not sure what integrated theory is, as applied to psychology and sociology, but in so far as I get a dull glimmer of comprehension as to what it might be, I feel rather sure that we do not have it, and hence the question of its applicability to teaching community organisation would seem to be somewhat premature.[1]

1. Roland Warren, 'Application of social science knowledge to the community organisation field', paper presented at the Annual Program Meeting of the Council for Social Work Education, Salt Lake City, January 1967. An edited version of this paper has since been published in the *Journal of Education for Social Work*, vol. 3, no. 1, Spring 1967.

But within the general criteria for selection discussed in the preceding chapter various alternative approaches are possible, for example:

1. To select one social science discipline for intensive study. This could both provide the student with a firm base in one area of relevant knowledge and develop the objectivity in observation and analysis on which social science rests and which is an essential component of community work.
2. To base the teaching on a problem-centred approach, as several social scientists suggested to us. A range of knowledge from the social sciences might be used to increase understanding of major or characteristic social problems with which the community worker was likely to be concerned in such fields as housing, poverty, physical disability and disablement, mental health, delinquency, education, immigration, old age, child care, youth, etc. This teaching should be closely linked with the similar teaching of community work method suggested on pp. 123–4.
3. To start with the problems as perceived by the students both initially and as the course progressed and to build interdisciplinary teaching around the exploration of these problems.
4. To integrate elements of scientific knowledge drawn from a variety of disciplines and applied to typical problems and tasks of community work.
5. To focus teaching on certain basic concepts from the social sciences such as cultural norms and values, status, class, role, groups and personality, and on scientific method.

Educationally there are strong arguments for these latter approaches but if they are to avoid superficiality and incoherence they make heavy demands on flexibility of course organisation and teaching ability. The gradual modification of teaching along traditional subject divisions by regular discussion amongst subject teachers to relate different concepts to each other would be a practical immediate aim. This should include construction of course syllabuses in the light of their relevance to the tasks of community work, with an interdisciplinary approach, and starting with issues significant to the students.

PRINCIPLES AND METHODS OF COMMUNITY WORK

The problems faced by the community worker derive from or involve the relationship between social institutions and human behaviour. While knowledge from sociology, social anthropology, social psychology, economics and other disciplines is necessary for the study, diagnosis and planning aspects of community work, the work itself involves much more than analytic ability, since like any professional practice it includes not only knowledge but also skills and attitudes. The worker is concerned to bring about beneficial change and this inevitably involves interaction with individuals and groups. Since community workers are constantly in group situations where their purpose is to influence such beneficial change, it is essential for them to have a good theoretical understanding of group interaction and dynamics and to be able to use this understanding in practice.[1] Even in reasonably normal groups they will sometimes have to work with difficult and disruptive individuals. In some neighbourhoods where there is much deviance, apathy or group conflict they may also carry a social therapy role where a good deal of understanding of the dynamics of individual and group behaviour will be necessary. The importance of such knowledge is not confined to understanding the individuals and groups with whom the worker is in contact at whatever level. He must also understand his own motivations and prejudices. Psychology can contribute to the self-understanding and self-awareness of the worker and thus to his disciplined use of himself, which is an essential requirement for skill in community work as distinct from personal flair. As we have also said in chapters 7 and 9, sociology too can contribute to this by enabling the worker to gain an understanding of his social position and its possible consequences for himself and for those with whom he works.

The community worker is essentially a practitioner, and training for community work, in addition to providing background knowledge, must attempt to develop within the student some general body of principles and methods relevant to his roles and work and (other than in short courses) to help the student to apply these in practice through supervised fieldwork. Although these principles and methods are essentially oriented towards practical action they are necessarily formulated here in generalised terms. For despite the fact that many people are involved in various types of community work, the principles on which they operate and the methods they use have only been conceptualised to a limited extent in this country. Even if it were possible to be more specific, it would be undesirable to focus training too narrowly, for the student will face a variety of situations in his subsequent work, many of which cannot be anticipated. In addition, he must be able to perceive and respond to major change and will need to make use of new knowledge from the social sciences as it becomes available. At the present stage of development too clearcut a definition of the work would be limiting. Moreover the purpose of training is to give students sound principles of analysis and practice rather than simply to teach factual knowledge and techniques.

A course in principles and methods aims to clarify a theory of

1. See chapter 9, p. 107; also Joan Matthews, *Working with Youth Groups*, University of London Press, 1966.

practice. It is concerned with action, both change and conservation, as well as with description, analysis and explanation. It makes use of but is driven to go beyond available social science theory. It also makes certain value assumptions which must be explicitly considered. And it relies heavily on accumulated experience, wisdom, intuition and flair. The general objective of such teaching is to equip students for better community work practice. In whatever degree of detail it is taught and however it is related to practice, such a course would include a general analytic description of community work, its nature and social context, the principles on which it is based and the auspices under which it is practised. A specimen syllabus is given in appendix D.

As has been said in another context in chapter 9, it is for community work practitioners and teachers to develop a theory of practice for themselves, borrowing fruitful concepts from the social sciences and social philosophy and adding their own recorded and analysed experience. This is constantly done by the teaching profession, by caseworkers, and indeed by doctors, engineers and others in their respective spheres.

TEACHING COMMUNITY WORK IN RELATION TO SPECIFIC SOCIAL PROBLEMS

One approach to the teaching of method would be to consider the application of community work to particular social problems or to the tasks of particular social services.

The list of possible topics could be extended almost indefinitely but might include: housing and redevelopment, analysis of the structure, organisation and needs of regional populations, socially deprived areas, rural areas, race relations, education, health and medical care, mental health, physical handicap, children, youth, the aged, delinquency.

Clearly it would not be possible in any course of reasonable length to cover all such topics. Some in-service training courses might be solely concerned with only one of them. It is desirable that students should have the opportunity to apply the principles and methods of community work to a specific problem or problems of significant social importance. Selection of topics would depend on the general criteria on p. 120, together with the probable future employment of the students and the opportunities available in students' field experience, or the emphasis in current social developments.

There is no intention to imply a standard pattern of training. The uncertainties and early stage of development of community work and the uneven knowledge on which it is based would preclude any such claim. Experiment and variation in approach are desirable, provided they are based on sound educational methods.

Within the foregoing framework, there is scope for different aspects either to be dealt with at an elementary level or to be given detailed treatment. In particular, training with more specific objectives, or students with special needs or interests, might require a modification of the suggested content or the addition of other subjects, such as aspects of the law. This might apply to the whole of a particular course, for example, with emphasis on the youth service or adult education methods, or there might be optional studies related to the interests of individual students. Depending on the background of the students and the length of the course, it might be possible to eliminate all or part of some of the background subjects, thus leaving greater scope for studies beyond the core content. Possibilities of providing for the special interest of individual students or groups of students would be increased if joint teaching could be arranged with other courses for caseworkers, teachers, medical students, administrators, lawyers, town planners, etc.

VARIOUS METHODS OF PRESENTATION AND STUDY

A variety of methods can provide appropriate learning experiences to enable students to assimilate and utilise the content of training. Such methods can be used in varying degrees in relation to various aspects of different types of course but are particularly relevant to the application of background knowledge to the tasks and problems of community work through the study of principles and methods of practice. Field experience is crucial because the aim is the development of appropriate attitudes and skills as well as the assimilation of knowledge. This is discussed in the next chapter. The following are possible methods of presentation in the classroom:

1. A combination of lecture and discussion in which the teacher both presents material and helps students to discuss it.
2. Visiting lecturers. People active in some aspect of community work who are brought in to speak about and discuss their own activities. Their contribution may be to speak from current practical experience about matters being studied by the students or they may be outstanding practitioners or people engaged in work of particular interest or of a pioneering nature. The number of such talks should be limited and must be fitted into a total framework.
3. Seminar or group discussions.
4. Presentation of material by students either individually or as groups. This material might be derived from a variety of sources – the training course, personal experience, private study or field experience.
5. Guided reading.

6. Written work. This could include a variety of other written material in addition to essays and sometimes dissertations. For example, reports; memoranda; background papers; minutes; applications; proposals; reports of group or committee meetings or interviews; summaries of books, government reports, research studies; and group projects as well as individual written work.
7. Individual and group tutorials.
8. Community work studies. A variety of case records either kept in the normal course of community work or specially prepared for study purposes would be useful. They could include records produced by students during their own field experience, as well as records edited for teaching purposes. In addition to written records, verbal presentations either by students or by participants in a community work situation, films, tape recordings of interviews or meetings can be effective. By the imaginative use of such materials any aspect of the processes and tasks of community work could be studied in detail and in slow motion.
9. Skills exercises. Some of the more specific skills or techniques used in community work, particularly those involved in study, analysis and communication, can be learned to some extent in the classroom, for example, the use of audio-visual aids.
10. Simulation exercises. Various aspects of community work practice can be simulated in the classroom through projects of various kinds, group exercises, specially designed case studies, role-playing, 'in-tray' exercises and so on.
11. Periodic recapitulation of material in class sessions.

These methods are interrelated and can be used in various combinations. Each is more effective for some learning purposes than others, more appropriate at some phases of training than others, more useful in some training circumstances than others. They should be used in ways which increase capacity for independent study, ability to grasp and use orderly methods of fact gathering, analysis, classification and concept formulation, in short, helping students to think to some purpose in relation to the content of the course. The criterion must always be the extent to which various methods contribute to the development by the student of the knowledge, attitudes and skills which it is the purpose of training to bring about.

Within this perspective, it will be obvious that particular techniques, however useful, should not be considered in isolation from the purposes, content and organisation of the training as a whole. Students learn from the total climate and activities of the course as well as from more formal teaching. This climate comprises many elements, but three are particularly important: the attitudes and behaviour of the teaching staff; the attitudes and behaviour of the student group; and the extent to which the content, methods of teaching and organisation of the training demonstrate in practice what is being taught in theory. Training itself should exemplify the knowledge, attitudes and skills it is attempting to impart so that the whole experience of the course contributes to the learning process. In training for community work this implies that it would be both consistent and profitable to involve the students as much as possible in the planning and organisation of the course.

The theoretical study and fieldwork teaching should be closely interwoven; both are important in the total assessment of student performance and the latter will therefore not be discussed until the end of the following chapter on fieldwork.

11

Proposed Content of Training: Practice: The Final Assessment of Students' Performance

THE PURPOSE OF FIELDWORK

Theory and practice have been separated for the purposes of discussion but in all substantial community work courses they must be parallel parts of the curriculum to enable students to relate theory and practice to each other. As in the preceding two chapters, the following discussion takes as its starting-point the demands of full time qualifying courses. But the principles apply elsewhere; for example, in-service training courses would draw upon the members' practical experience, thus sandwich courses on the lines of the National Council of Social Service and the National Institute for Social Work Training pioneer experiments (see chapter 5, p. 57) include observation, together with analysis of the members' own practice. The inclusion of some community work in the training of caseworkers, youth leaders, teachers and others would be – indeed is being – based upon essentially the same principles applied in their particular fields. The purpose of field-work is to enable students to perceive in real life what they are studying theoretically, to apply this knowledge in order to acquire skill as community workers, and in doing so to develop more awareness of themselves and others, coupled with the appropriate attitudes and values. The main emphasis in this chapter is on grass roots and direct agency experience, though, again, the same principles would apply to fieldwork at the wider planning, negotiating, policy decision level.

The effectiveness of supervised field experience will depend on the opportunities available, the extent to which they can be improved and the objectives of the course of which the field experience is part. The general aims are to enable students to have:

1. Experience of working in an organisation undertaking community work.
2. Knowledge and experience of a particular community, its problems and the organisations working in it.
3. Knowledge and experience of some of the social needs and forms of social provision with which community work is concerned.
4. Opportunities for the application of knowledge and principles to actual community situations.
5. Opportunities to develop the skills and techniques necessary for effective community work.
6. Opportunities to develop self-awareness and a disciplined use of

the student's own personality as a helper in a variety of community work situations, flexibility of response to many different people and situations, as well as clarity about aims.

OBSERVATION AND STUDY OF COMMUNITY SITUATIONS

Fieldwork includes visits of observation to a variety of organisations engaged in some form of community work in its broadest sense; observation of, or participation in, certain activities such as committee and other meetings; field studies of particular communities and of specific social needs and forms of social provision; discussions with fieldworkers, community leaders, participants in community efforts and the clients of services; experience of the processes involved in community work such as fact-finding, recording, report writing, budgeting and so on. These varied experiences need to be carefully planned in relation to the academic content of the course and to each other. They should be well prepared for, adequately recorded and subsequently discussed and related to the general work of the course.[1]

THE RANGE OF FIELD EXPERIENCE

Observation, participation in and study of community situations and processes provide an appropriate beginning to field experience and remain a continuing element in fieldwork. But it is a prelude to the development of skill for which the student must be supervised in the actual practice of community work. The totality of field experience varies in length and degree of involvement or responsibility along some such continuum as the following:

1. Single observations, e.g. attendance at a committee meeting, a staff discussion, an inter-organisational discussion, or a public meeting of an immigrants association.
2. More sustained observation and study, e.g. a short placement in an agency engaged in some form of community work.
3. Undertaking a specific and limited task as assistant to a community worker, e.g. collecting and analysing information, drafting a memorandum or report, recruiting people into a voluntary service scheme.
4. Assuming responsibility for one phase or aspect of a project or community work process, e.g. gathering and presenting information concerning a community problem or need to an agency, working party or committee.

1. Many of the issues involved in fieldwork of this type are discussed in 'Field Work with Muintir na Tire: An Assessment of a Six Year Experiment', R. A. B. Leaper, Symposium on Community Development Training, Zwolle, the Netherlands, mimeographed, 1967.

5. Taking a sustained responsibility for a community work task, e.g. planning and implementing a particular development or project with a staff or inter-agency group; bringing together a group of mothers, helping them to decide what they want to do and assisting them to implement their decisions – such as establishing a pre-school playgroup.

All forms of field experience need careful planning and preparation. If they are to be really useful, students must report back and discuss their findings and these experiences must be related to the whole content of the course.

PATTERNS OF FIELD EXPERIENCE

In the first part of a course, field experience might consist of specific tasks, visits of observation, and short placements as suggested above with the emphasis on observation, participation and study rather than community work practice. They provide a basis for later field placements with responsibility. They are also valuable in a different way for students with previous community work experience. There would also be advantages in delaying the first placement for actual practice rather than observation until the student was firmly established on the course and had built up some background of knowledge.

No single or standard pattern of field experience can be formulated and there is room for experiment and the assessment of various patterns. A course lasting two years or more would have more options than a one-year course which would be working within much more severe limits and might only be able to have one major practice placement of some four to five months duration during the second and third terms, preceded by short periods of field observation and study during the first term. This field experience might usefully be extended by a block placement of two or three months after the end of the academic year.

AGENCIES FOR SUPERVISED FIELD PRACTICE

In order to provide in supervised field practice for the interests and needs of particular students and to prepare them for different subsequent careers, a course should aim to develop placements in as wide a variety of agencies as possible, in terms of purposes, auspices, organisations, method of work, activities, size of operation, type of area and clientele, nature of problems dealt with and so on. This would also enrich class discussion and the collective experience of the student group.

The selection of particular agencies for field training would depend on: the standard of work of the agency; the opportunities it is able to offer for practice and learning relevant to the purposes of the course; the agency's interest in student training and ability to offer such necessary facilities as skilled staff, time, space, etc.; common aims in the approach and methods of the agency and of the course, and the possibility of developing close working relationships.

FIELDWORK TEACHERS

It is essential for an agency to be able to make suitable fieldwork teachers (sometimes called supervisors) available. Considerations would be the field teachers' personality, knowledge, skill and experience, their teaching ability, their position in the agency, the time they can make available, and their readiness to cooperate with the training course.

Their responsibilities would include:

1. Planning and making the necessary arrangements. This would include introducing the students to the policies, procedures and work of the agency as a whole and its social context; the selection or creation from among the various activities of the agency of learning opportunities appropriate to the student's training needs and the time available; and helping the student to plan his use of time in the field.
2. The development of the student's skill in community work through supervised field practice.
3. Evaluation of the student's performance in the field, including his achievements, limitations and potential capacity for community work, and the submission of written reports to the staff of the course.

Field teachers with these capacities will not be found ready made. They will have to be created, as has happened elsewhere, by those in charge of the course running seminars for them which include the skills of field teaching as well as orienting them to the theoretical content of the curriculum. In the present dearth of field teachers it will be necessary for the courses to have additional staff able to give substantial time to work with inexperienced supervisors as well as with students about their fieldwork. These sessions with supervisors are also an effective form of in-service training and a valuable contribution by the educational institution to the work of the agency.

Close collaboration is thus essential between the fieldwork teacher and those responsible for the course. This will include regular consultation with the course teachers about the student's work and progress as well as participation in meetings and seminars arranged for fieldwork teachers.

SELECTION OF FIELDWORK

There should be careful matching of the individual student and the agency in his own interests as well as that of the field agency. It is desirable to take into account:

1. His previous training and experiences, including experience on the course.
2. His probable level of performance.
3. His interests and intentions regarding future work.
4. His learning needs as assessed on the course and revealed by any previous field training.
5. Whether he and the fieldwork teacher are likely to be able to work fruitfully together.

Fieldwork teachers should be provided in advance with information about the student's educational background and previous experience, performance on the course and other relevant details. Students also should be given both a general and individual preparation for field training so that they understand its purpose and place in the total course, the relationship between the course teachers and fieldwork teachers, the experience they will be given, the skill they are expected to acquire and the nature, purpose and use of evaluation reports on their performance.

THE STUDENTS' FIELDWORK EXPERIENCE

During the initial period in the agency the student should familiarise himself sufficiently with it to be able to begin work and feel sufficiently at ease to question, express ideas, take advantage of the opportunities the agency offers and generally to learn from his field experience.

Appropriate opportunities should be taken to involve the student in a broad range of activity, including attendance at and participation in committee meetings, staff meetings, discussions with other agencies and the allocation of *ad hoc* tasks which are useful in themselves and helpful to the student in gaining a wider experience of the agency's work. These experiences should be systematically discussed with him.

Valuable as such wide ranging activities and involvement may be, it is essential for the student to have a more concentrated and sustained experience of practice. He should have real responsibility for one or more definite pieces of work which he conducts on a relatively self-directing basis. This will be the crux of the fieldwork experiences, and by far the most difficult to provide. Possibilities include: stimulating interest in some local issue; house to house visiting for some purpose; bringing together a few people with a common problem or interest; assisting a community group in its day-to-day operations; developing some special project such as a summer programme for children; helping a given community service to be in more effective contact with the needs of its clientele or neighbourhood; participating in a service agency's reorganisation of some part of its operation; starting a new aspect of its services; assisting in the development of relations between the agency and other organisations and community groups; servicing a joint study or planning group of agency representatives.

The difficulty is to shape the many possibilities into practice tasks which are feasible for the agency and will also help the students to develop skills. Fieldwork teachers and the staff of a course must work very closely together in discussing, planning and implementing these field experiences. Sometimes a student may be able to carry considerable independent responsibility for work; more often he will be an assistant or partner to the fieldwork teacher or other responsible staff member of the agency, as it will often be difficult to delimit tasks and there will usually be a need to ensure continuity. In order to broaden the student's experience as well as ensure against unforeseen or unpredictable developments, he should carry responsibility for more than one piece of work.

In field practice the student must develop skill in the two interrelated activities which are the essence of community work. First, study, including fact-finding, observation and analysis of social situations and processes and the drawing of conclusions, making recommendations and developing plans on the basis of this material. Second, forming effective working relationships with people, individually, in groups, in organisations, as representatives and so on, with the dual purpose of understanding situations and making relationships in order to bring about change.

Supervision has both administrative and educational components. Administratively it must ensure that the agency's work is carried out adequately and thus safeguard the agency in accepting students to work in it. Educationally, the field experience should help the student to grow in competence.

It is essential for the student to have regular supervisory sessions of about one or two hours a week. The fieldwork teacher must also be available for discussion and guidance on urgent issues as they arise. The student must be enabled to discuss freely the situations and problems with which he is faced, the carrying out of the tasks which he has been allocated, and his own performance. The fieldwork teacher must be able to help the student to relate theoretical knowledge, past experience and the principles and methods of community work to the current situation and to examine and assess his field experience objectively, including his own attitudes and responses. The aim is to help the student to develop greater understanding of the people and situations in which he is involved, more effective approaches and methods of working, and greater self-awareness and self-discipline so that he may gain competence in accomplishing particular tasks. The emphasis in supervision should be positive and focused on the development of the student's skill and improved performance in the field rather than negatively critical and directive. This would include studying the student's records and other written materials and making notes of supervisory sessions as a means of understanding his personality, needs and patterns of learning. These notes are also a basis for planning and for evaluation reports.

Detailed recording by the student of at least some aspects of his field experience is an essential part of fieldwork. Some recording in the form of completion of agency records, progress reports, minutes, correspondence, memoranda, proposals, etc., will almost certainly be required for the agency's work. Such records are a part of and can be used in training. More detailed recording, both of events and of the student's part in them, and his perceptions of and thinking and feeling about what happened, is also necessary. Such recording helps to develop increased understanding of the processes of human interaction besides helping the fieldwork teacher to work with the student and assess his needs and progress. Records may take the form of a continuous narrative record of the development of a particular piece of work; more detailed process records of certain interviews, a meeting of a community group, a committee meeting, a staff meeting, a joint meeting with another agency, etc.; a summary of development or work over a period of time; a diary or log book of all the student's activity in the agency; or various combinations of these.

The course will need records of field experience for study in the classroom and this must be taken into account in deciding on the kind of records required of students.

REPORTS ON STUDENTS' FIELDWORK

Student's records also contribute usefully to the total evidence for the fieldwork teacher's written evaluation of the student's progress. Such evaluations should be written in a form and according to criteria agreed between the course teachers and the field supervisors. In addition to a description of the responsibilities allocated to the student, an assessment must be made of the level of performance attained by him at the end of the placement. The report might include:

General attitudes, abilities and behaviour as revealed in the placement.

Performance as a worker in the agency and in contacts with other agencies. Ability in recording and other administrative processes.

Skills in processes involved in community work. Ability to use knowledge and to apply theory to practice.

134

Ability to engage in a systematic process of problem solving and to anticipate the probable consequences of various lines of action.

Ability to stimulate and sustain people's action in relation to a problem or task, to be able to encourage positive relationships among individuals, groups and organisations, to foster interorganisational cooperation, and to help problem solving groups to function.

Ability to accept hostility and to deal with conflict.

Ability to understand community structure and processes and to analyse the interplay of people and forces in a community situation.

Appreciation of realistic factors in a given situation.

Understanding of social forces, social policies and social provisions as they affect specific community situations and problems.

Self-awareness (including culturally determined attitudes), sensitivity to the reactions of others, and a capacity for disciplined use of his own personality. Ability to identify with professional standards and behaviour and to act professionally by filling roles appropriate to different situations, including the use he has made of supervision.

Main strengths and weaknesses as revealed in the placement, and special needs for the next placement or the first job.

These generalised aspects may require modification in relation to the actual opportunities offered by a particular placement. In their reports fieldwork teachers should give factual evidence for their assessments, citing examples from the student's practice. A comprehensive report along such lines as these should be required on completion of each placement.

The written evaluations are used in the final assessment of students. Although in the last resort they must therefore represent the best judgement of the fieldwork teacher, they should grow out of the supervisory sessions and contribute to the student's training and development through an examination with him of his own experience and performance. Evaluation should be a continuing element in supervision, so that when a written evaluation comes to be made its contents should be no surprise to the student.

LENGTH AND TYPE OF PLACEMENT

If, as suggested, field placements are to provide opportunities for the sustained practice of community work as distinguished from observation, participation and study, they must be of sufficient length for this purpose. No firm generalisation can be made about their desirable length, partly because there is insufficient knowledge and experience on which to base generalisations and partly because of the many practical and educational factors involved.

Ideally, it would seem that the longer the placement the more opportunities it could offer students to see work through from

135

beginning to end, but the work of some agencies may go in cycles, and phases of the work might well be of limited length. There will probably be natural breaks in the work of the agency such as the summer holidays, while the length of the commitment into which supervisors can enter will be limited. In addition, there may be diminishing returns from some placements in relation to the specific training needs of the student. It may even be possible for a student to accept considerable responsibility for a specific and time-limited project on a quite short placement of, say, a month.

Limits will be set to the period of the placement by the total length of the course and by the balance between classwork and fieldwork. It will also be affected by decisions concerning the pattern and number of placements. In community organisation training in the U.S.A. students have traditionally spent the full academic year in one placement but there is a move towards a more flexible pattern. By analogy with casework training in this country, a three months' block, i.e. full time, or a six months' concurrent placement would be desirable.

In concurrent placements the week is split between classwork and fieldwork, which offers the best opportunity for relating and integrating theory and practice though it may cause strain for the student. And it is not easy to ensure that what is being experienced in fieldwork runs parallel with what is being taught in the classroom. In addition, it may be extremely difficult to confine community work practice to certain days of each week. To do so may further limit the field experience which can be offered to students and make it more difficult for them to be accepted as temporary members of the agency able to carry real responsibility.

For community work practice, therefore, block placements may have some advantages to both agency and student. The main disadvantage is that a block placement breaks the continuity of classwork and tends to divorce theory and practice more radically. It also shortens the period of fieldwork thus making it more difficult for the student to experience a complete phase of work, for typical community work tasks tend to be spaced irregularly over a long period with spurts of considerable activity which are followed by relative quiescence, while developments often take some time to come to fruition.

Possibly some combination of concurrent and block placements or some form of modified block placements might offer a solution. This might, for example, take the form of four days a week in the agency and one in the university or college, or five days a week in the agency with a block period of, say, three days of classwork at about four-weekly intervals.

A further consideration affecting fieldwork placements is the number of placements needed to develop the necessary range and depth of skill. Every student's experience should include both the grass roots and inter-agency aspects of community work.[1]

POSSIBLE DEVELOPMENTS

The field training of social caseworkers provides the most systematically developed model and the most relevant experience for field training of community workers; indeed community fieldwork is beginning to be developed in casework courses, as we have shown in chapter 5. But field training in casework is still developing and experimenting.

One current advance is the establishment of student units, that is to say a group of students working in one agency often though not always with the same field teacher. This is attractive both educationally and from the point of view of making the most economical use of scarce field teaching resources. It does not wholly replace individual supervision, but a good deal of teaching can be done in the group, while the group itself offers a valuable learning situation for the student. This device is particularly relevant to community work, even though a student unit sometimes isolates the students from the normal demands and pressures of the agency. Also, owing to the small scale of many existing community work operations, it might be difficult to find real responsibilities for a group of students for a substantial period. Both these difficulties would be less important if the student unit were not confined within a single agency but used a variety of field experiences.

The chief obstacle to expanding satisfactory training is the shortage of experienced field teachers and the difficulty of maintaining standards and ensuring appropriate experience when the supervisor is employed by the agency and is primarily responsible for carrying out its work, often with insufficient time for training students. An alternative is for the educational institution to employ the fieldwork teacher and attach him or her to an agency with responsibility for student supervision. This close association between particular agencies and training courses could result in a fruitful exchange of theoretical knowledge and local experience. Another alternative is for an educational institution to develop its own field operations either in the form of an agency or of special field projects. Such developments make it easier to plan the students' programme as a coherent whole and to relate theory and practice more closely. The danger is that in doing this it will undermine the essential value of field experience by making it more academic and less practical. On the other hand, if there were skilled practitioners on the staff of the

1. There is useful material in *A Curriculum Outline in Community Work*, Israel Ministry of Social Welfare, Institute for Training Social Workers, Jerusalem, 1965, especially pp. 58–60 and 62–6.

course with a clear educational responsibility it would be possible to relax requirements otherwise necessary to ensure that students' training needs are met. For example, it might no longer be essential to insist that students should be placed where they would be under the educational supervision of an experienced worker. A greater range of field experience might be used in field training with the educational responsibility resting with the fieldwork teacher provided by the educational institution. The fieldwork teacher would be a full member of the course staff and thus able to ensure integration of classwork and fieldwork. This division of educational and administrative responsibility, however, poses problems for both the agency and the educational institution which would have to be carefully considered.

If these two possibilities could be satisfactorily worked out, local training units could be started, consisting of a member of the teaching staff and a group of students, and using a range of field experience in the area. The unit might create such opportunities itself by developing particular projects or it might use opportunities in community work agencies, in a range of other organisations, and in more informal situations in the community such as an autonomous neighbourhood group. The whole range of possible field experiences from single observation through to sustained community work practice might be used flexibly to provide fruitful learning experiences for students. But it would be essential to give coherence and depth to what could otherwise easily become scattered and superficial pieces of experience.

Student field experience might, for example, be organised round three aspects:

1. Knowledge and understanding of communities – their structure and functioning, needs and provisions. The physical environment and its effect on social relationships and use of social resources; local government and political life; the social services; voluntary organisations including those of consumer or cause types.
2. Working directly with people in a community, including, for example, home visiting to inform people about some service, or to recruit them into organisations or activities, or making contact, e.g. with young people in the streets, pubs, coffee bars, etc.; forming a group or subgroup of an association; helping members of a group to explore, become articulate about and select issues and problems for action; observing or participating in negotiations, including conflict situations.
3. Working in service and planning organisations including, for example, experience of different activities such as discussions, training; experience of committees – observation and participation; experience of administration including preparation of

proposals and public interpretation; participation in research activities – gathering and analysing data; participation in inter-agency activities with opportunities for contacts with people at different levels in administrative hierarchies.

The field experience of students and others could be utilised in the teaching, and the classwork would include community work studies, skill teaching and simulation exercises. Classwork and fieldwork would thus overlap, and the development of field training units would increase such overlap. The fieldwork continuum could become in a real sense a classwork fieldwork continuum.

ASSESSMENT OF STUDENTS' TOTAL PERFORMANCE IN THE THEORY AND PRACTICE ELEMENTS OF THE COURSE

Assessment of the student's performance in various aspects of the theoretical studies and field training, covering the interrelated aspects of knowledge, skill and attitudes, should be a continuing part of the course, undertaken in close collaboration with the student. All training staff in contact with the students should play a part – subject teachers, field supervisors, and the student's individual tutor or tutors – as well as the student himself. The materials available might include: written work during the course; examination scripts, special projects involving analytical and relationship skills; records of performance and progress during training; field teachers' and class teachers' reports.

The number of qualified and experienced people involved in producing or assessing this material and the views of the external examiners should be a reasonable safeguard against bias or subjectivity. Except in some types of in-service training, a systematic and standardised procedure will usually be required for the final assessment.

The major problems of assessment are:

1. Defining the aspects of performance to be assessed in sufficiently concrete terms to establish standards or norms of performance.
2. Devising methods or instruments of assessment which are sufficiently relevant, objective and reliable.
3. Assessing progress during training and level of performance at the end of training.
4. The difficulty of weighing or balancing various aspects of performance in order to arrive at a general assessment.

Assessment should have some reference to performance subsequent to training as well as during or at the end of training. It is also important to be constantly aware of the bad effect on students' performance of inappropriate forms of assessment.

The way forward is by a vigorous attempt to define the objectives of training in concrete terms of knowledge and behaviour and by the development of methods of assessment which truly reflect performance in these. Nonetheless there are no absolute standards of achievement and the problem of deciding what is an acceptable level of performance in the different aspects of the course will still remain. The temptation to overteach is an ever present reminder that a little done well is better than much done poorly. It is most desirable that the teaching staffs of different courses should come together from time to time to pool experience and undertake controlled experiments in various aspects of the course content, the teaching, and the means used to assess students' achievements.

Conclusions

Conclusions

12
Next Steps

In drawing together our conclusions and relating them to practical issues of implementation we must emphasise that fragmentation of policy and practice arising from the present organisation of government, both centrally and locally, as well as diverse voluntary efforts could easily nullify the objectives and training proposals set out in this report.

We have constantly stressed the importance of a more coherent approach to people, their needs and their social conditions, and that the essential purpose of all community work is to enable people to play a more effective part in social affairs. Community work at its various levels must have an essentially integrative role so far as the operation of services is concerned whether the purpose is to reduce apathy or alienation or to enable planners and policy makers to become more aware of common human needs. It would, however, be unrealistic to imagine that a greater degree of integration of services would automatically result from new forms and content of training or new types of job. And, as we have stressed elsewhere, better coordinated services must not be confused with attempts to produce some all-embracing community harmony. The reality of conflicting interests cannot be ignored, nor the need to give more active help and support to those least able to meet their own needs in the community.

THE NEED FOR COORDINATED PLANNING

A major effort is required to overcome piecemeal planning in the execution of community policies. The next few years offer a unique opportunity for fresh thinking about these problems as a result of the reviews which are currently taking place of the civil service, local government structure, the reorganisation of the local authority and allied personal social services and the administration of the national health service. Growing dissatisfaction with the present machinery of government may also lead to a more fundamental review of the whole system of central administration. The recent government move which could lead to the ultimate formation of a Ministry of Social Welfare is significant in this context.

In this fluid and complex situation community planning, and consequently the training of planners, is bound to become more relevant as planning techniques improve. We have tried to identify certain functions, some of which already exist, and others which need to be made explicit, in order to ensure that a more comprehensive approach is made to planning in a society in which change and conservation must be kept in balance, where well-informed consent and the appropriate participation of citizens must be sought in the development of social policy.

We shall have good cause for satisfaction if our report contributes to the achievement of a greater degree of interdepartmental and statutory/voluntary cooperation and coordination in matters of immense importance. In addition to the discussions which we suggest on p. 145 about our training proposals, a modest but important start in this wider process could be made through a series of consultations and short courses which would bring together policy makers, both nationally and locally, whose departmental policies are clearly related in their impact on communities. The policies of many central government departments indeed have implicit within them ideas similar to those developed in this report. There is a need, however, for much more interdepartmental consultation about the means by which common policies for social development might be implemented. The first move must come from the Ministers concerned.

The Social Work (Scotland) Act 1968 and the awaited publication of the Report of the Seebohm Committee, together with the Reports of the Mallaby and Maud Committees provide a challenging opportunity to reorganise the provision of local social services. We very much hope that two-way communication with local groups and communities will be built into the reorganised services and that every effort will be made to stimulate the recruitment and training of suitable staff.

Both central and local government need to review the education and training of those who play a major part in formulating and executing social policies. Chapter 2 refers to new provisions for introducing administrative civil servants to studies in social policy and social administration and chapter 5 to similar efforts being made for senior local government officers by the Institute of Local Government Studies at the University of Birmingham. The new course in social service administration at the University of Essex is also interesting.[1] The newly established Local Government Training Board should stimulate further courses of training for senior and middle grade staff in local government.

It is obviously a big step for organisations whose traditions have not included recognition of community work functions to review their policies, redefine tasks, recruit staff, and spend money on

1. This course, which starts in October 1968, will give preference for the first two years to candidates employed in local authority welfare departments. Thereafter it will be open to candidates in other central or local government social services.

training in a type of work which is relatively new. Careful evaluation of such innovations will be essential.

Some experiments might also be made in the training and employment of special staff to carry out functions of interdepartmental or inter-agency planning whose contribution and responsibility would be to reflect the needs of communities and their responses to new policies and provisions. Training for such posts needs to be planned at a high level in relation to such employment opportunities as exist or might be brought into existence.

We cannot afford to dissipate scarce resources through uncoordinated and duplicated services and training schemes. Vigorous steps must be taken to reduce the danger of dissipation which results from the sheer number of statutory departments, voluntary organisations, educational institutions and professional bodies which have a say in the administration of the relevant services.

FINANCIAL IMPLICATIONS OF TRAINING PROGRAMMES

The development of training courses must inevitably depend on the teaching resources available and on willingness to invest money and staff in this type of education and training. We hope that the training issues raised in this report will be fully considered by the relevant government departments, the local authority associations and the universities, the Local Government Training Board, the various advisory and training councils in the social work and educational fields, and relevant voluntary and professional organisations. A number of small conferences for representatives of the various interests concerned could usefully consider the training implications of our report and decide upon further action.

Many people in the social and educational services are aware of the need for community workers and training courses. But without money neither employment nor training will become available. These financial implications are the concern of more than one government department as well as of local authorities and voluntary organisations.

There is no reason in principle why university courses in community work should not be financed through the University Grants Committee and other courses through the Department of Education and Science and local education authorities, although, in the present economic situation, special measures may be necessary until courses are well established. Provision is made for this in Scotland under the Social Work (Scotland) Act 1968.[1]

1. The principle embodied in the *Report of the Royal Commission on Medical Education*, para 195, is also worth consideration in our context.

THE NEED FOR A NATIONAL COUNCIL TO PROMOTE TRAINING FOR COMMUNITY WORK

Our training proposals will not be effectively implemented unless they are the specific responsibility of a national training council, though it is clearly undesirable that yet another separate council should be set up when too many exist already. At present various national training and/or advisory bodies span the fields of social work, the youth service and adult education. It is likely that in time the number of these bodies will be reduced through amalgamation and expansion, for example, in the field of social work. Meantime, however, it seems essential that all the main interests should be involved in the promotion of training for community work. The execution of our proposals would be in itself a major community planning task and would involve careful work by government officials, existing training and advisory councils and others in order to incorporate community work in a general structure.

Ideally we think it desirable that responsibility for the promotion of training for community work should be assumed by a statutory training council also responsible for training for all forms of social work and possibly the youth service and some aspects of adult education. As a first step towards this it may be desirable for the government to set up an independent committee or council to promote training for community work and consisting of representatives of the various national training and/or advisory bodies (including the Joint University Council for Social and Public Administration) together with some members from appropriate educational institutions and employer organisations, with an independent chairman and a small staff.

The purposes of a training council, whether in its interim or long-term form, would be promotion, coordination, and validation of standards. The first purpose would be to promote and regulate the growth of courses of training for full time community work; to secure extensive improvement, coordination of and assistance to many types of in-service training for community workers, members of other professions and voluntary workers. Other promotional purposes would include the production of teaching materials, providing information, promoting research and evaluation, and sponsoring short courses and consultations. Its coordination activities would include exchange of views with members of other professions related to community work, and consultations and discussions with employing authorities and relevant professional associations. The validation of standards would include arriving at agreed formulae for the recognition of courses, clarification of the nature and length of courses leading to professional recognition,

146

and conferring the qualifying award on students taking recognised full time courses in colleges of further education.

The council would need a well-qualified staff of sufficient standing. It should be an independent but publicly financed body. In the first stages it would probably be concerned to a considerable extent with in-service training for unqualified community workers, but as the number of full time qualifying courses increases this balance would begin to change.

New types of professional training can go unrecognised by traditional bodies. But we believe there is sufficient common interest among those organisations concerned with professional training to justify our hope that soundly planned training courses in community work will obtain early recognition. This recognition should follow fairly naturally if, as we propose in chapter 8, training for community work should become a stream within existing and well established patterns of training leading to the same award. Recognition from these quarters will help to ensure that good standards of selection, teaching and field practice are achieved and that limited resources are used to the best advantage. This is vital because the products of new or extended training programmes will be ambassadors of community work training.

A STRATEGY FOR THE USE OF SCARCE TEACHING RESOURCES

Community work may soon become so fashionable that educational institutions will be encouraged to establish training courses with inadequate facilities for theoretical teaching and field practice. To avert this danger, education and training in this field should at first be concentrated in a few university or other educational institutions in two or three areas. They should be able to depend largely on local resources, particularly in fieldwork. This would suggest that at the maximum two courses might be located in London, and two or three in all in Scotland, Wales and the provinces.

Additional impetus will be needed from a small number of employing authorities who are willing to participate in the experiment by providing both fieldwork and employment. These employing authorities should also play an important part in the evaluation of the outcome of training.

A useful experiment could be made with 'cadetships' or 'internships' under which a few newly qualified community workers spent, say, a year in appointments within easy reach of a community work course, so that under further field supervision and tutorial guidance they could consolidate their learning and skills effectively in a work situation. This would be particularly necessary for those who later go into pioneer appointments or become supervisors or community work teachers.

Teething troubles are likely to arise, since adaptations on the part of a newly trained worker, his colleagues and the organisation will be necessary, and these can sometimes be painful. There will be a natural tendency for some of the less experienced products of a new training to overlay their sense of being pioneers with the additional feeling of being crusaders. The reception of workers in these circumstances can be trying for senior officers and colleagues. To some extent this is a price to be paid for any new development but both teachers and employers will need to be in contact with each other if these problems are to be reduced. It can be equally trying for newly trained workers if their knowledge and skill are undervalued or rejected. Some of these tensions will exist for those trained at more senior policy and planning levels as well as for younger recruits.

In a total strategy of training it is as necessary to provide good in-service training for experienced workers including secondment to take qualifying courses as it is to pioneer professional training for new recruits. It is essential not to lose sight of the benefits of in-service training in community work, not only for the many untrained community workers but also for administrators, teachers, the clergy, caseworkers and others. Indeed this is likely to avoid or lessen some of the resistances mentioned above, since people would be returning to their own jobs not as strange new products but as administrative officers in various services, or head teachers, or child care or probation officers, who are able to bring new skills and understanding to their jobs. The aim should be to raise the whole standard of community work in all its forms. For this purpose a partnership must be developed between employing authorities, professional associations and educational institutions in order that each may learn from the other. This is dependent upon common understanding of the overall purposes, concepts and methods underlying all forms of community work. Through such a cooperative exercise between national training and advisory bodies, educational institutions, research workers, community workers, employing authorities and students it should be possible to develop and coordinate these experiments in controlled social change.

In this report it has been necessary to say a good deal about structures, staff, career prospects, the content of training and the like. But we conclude by reaffirming that these are only means to an end. The aim is the service of people so that they may live more happily, and that in a highly organised society there may be more rather than less scope for social democracy.

Summary

1. Community work includes: (*a*) helping local people to decide, plan and take action to meet their own needs with the help of available outside resources; (*b*) helping local services to become more effective, usable and accessible to those whose needs they are trying to meet; (*c*) taking account of the interrelation between different services in planning for people; (*d*) forecasting necessary adaptations to meet new social needs in constantly changing circumstances. Community work thus has in it aspects of direct neighbourhood work, closer relations between services and people, inter-agency coordination, and planning and policy formulation.

2. This community work function should be a recognised part of the professional practice of teachers, social workers, the clergy, health workers, architects, planners, administrators and others. In modern conditions of social change it is also a necessary full time professional task. Many different voluntary workers including local councillors are also active in community work.

3. The number of full time community workers (called by different titles) is increasing and rough estimates suggest that this is likely to continue. A comprehensive survey is necessary to clarify further the nature of their work in relation to the need for a career structure and salary scales. A detailed study of practice would also make an essential contribution to training (see also 12 below).

4. Community work method includes study of social situations and the use of relationships with groups and individuals for the purpose of bringing about some desirable social change.

5. It is important that community work should be undertaken by both public authorities and voluntary organisations. For certain purposes community workers can only be effective if they are within the power structure of the public services. On the other hand, independent organisations, including the churches, play a valuable role in community work through independent action or constructive protest whether in support of or in opposition to public authorities.

6. Voluntary work of all kinds is the essence of community life. This also points to the importance of support and training for volunteers. This is being fully explored by the Aves Committee and is therefore not discussed in this report.

F

7. Community work has in it elements of social work, adult education and administration. This must be taken into account in evolving a coherent pattern of training and in working out transfer from one career to another, with necessary additions to the original qualification.

8. It is urgent to expand in-service training for existing full time community workers, for voluntary workers and for social workers and youth leaders, the clergy, teachers, health workers, administrators and others who are now becoming more conscious of the community element in their work. Specific objectives and therefore the content and educational method of in-service training courses would vary considerably according to the participant's background and the length and purpose of the course. Local authority training officers, the Local Government Training Board, educational institutions, professional associations and a national council (see 15) should all actively contribute to the promotion of sound in-service training. Voluntary organisations will often need assistance either in planning their own courses or in sending people to take part in other courses.

9. It is equally important to start a few carefully planned full time courses of training for community work within existing patterns of training and leading to one of the generally recognised university or other qualifying awards. Much effort will be needed to provide adequate community work teaching and fieldwork on these pioneer courses. Student units are desirable for fieldwork. It is also essential that the first courses should have sufficient staff to supervise students, to give extra help to inexperienced field teachers, to collect and edit case records and other teaching material and to meet regularly for consultation about the content of the courses and student assessment. One year 'cadetships' or 'internships' near a course centre to enable newly qualified community workers to consolidate their skill under supervision would be an effective means of producing better qualified community workers, supervisors and teachers.

10. The social sciences, particularly sociology and psychology, underpin community work. They also provide much of the knowledge from which a theory of practice could emerge. The selection of subject matter from the social sciences and formulating the principles and practice of community work must be undertaken by community work teachers and practitioners in cooperation with social scientists and others.

11. Community work, like other professional activities, has in it the three elements of knowledge, skill and attitudes. Training must therefore include sufficient field practice to develop competence, ability to apply knowledge, and to work constructively with

groups and individuals, within a code of ethics to guard against the dangers of manipulation.

12. Continuing research, recording and analysis of practice, and evaluation of the relation of training to the needs of the field are all essential, both to the improvement of training and practice and also in due time to make advanced training possible. In particular, research should be built into each stage of certain in-service and full time training courses from the planning stage, through to students' subsequent performance in their first appointments (see also 3).

13. Relevant application of community studies should be part of the initial training of medical students, teachers, architects, administrators and others. It is also important that those who are assuming administrative, policy-making and planning responsibilities at later points in their career should take post-graduate courses which include community studies.

14. It is assumed that students training for full time community work could be grant-aided through the existing general provision. Courses in colleges of further education would be financed by local education authorities. University courses would no doubt come within general University Grants Committee provision. However, until they were well established they would have low priority compared with other pressing claims, thus special financing would be necessary for a time. An important role in full time and in-service training will be played by the Local Government Training Board and in Scotland through the new powers under the Social Work (Scotland) Act 1968.

15. A publicly financed but independent council should be responsible for all forms of training for community work. It should fulfil many functions within the general framework of promotion, coordination and validation of standards. It would, however, be most undesirable that this should become yet another specialised council. The aim should be one national council for all forms of social work, and possibly for the youth service and some aspects of adult education. As a first step the government might decide to set up an independent committee composed of all the interests concerned but with the intention that this would only be an interim measure.

16. It is hoped that there will be a series of consultations and conferences to discuss the foregoing conclusions, particularly in regard to the practice of community work, a career structure, and the development of full time and in-service training. The Social Work (Scotland) Act 1968 and the impending reports of the Seebohm Committee and the Royal Commissions on Local Government will make these discussions all the more timely.

Appendix A

Individuals who have given personal assistance to the Study Group

Miss Geraldine Aves, Chairman, Committee on Voluntary Workers in the Social Services.

Miss A. J. Bambra, Chelsea College of Physical Education, Eastbourne.

Miss Ilys Booker, North Kensington Family Study.

Mr G. Brooke Taylor, Social Relations Officer, Dawley New Town.

Mr David Buchanan, Folk House, Bristol.

Dr Wilfred Burns, City Planning Department, Newcastle upon Tyne.

Mr P. Buss, Burlington Hall Neighbourhood Centre, Birmingham.

Professor G. M. Carstairs, Department of Psychiatry, University of Edinburgh.

Professor T. E. Chester, Department of Social Administration, University of Manchester.

Mr R. T. Clarke, Yorkshire Council of Social Service.

Mr David Collett, Blackfriars Federation of Settlements.

Professor Cotgrove, School of Humanities and Social Sciences, Bath University of Technology.

Mr and Mrs Oliver Cox, Shankland, Cox and Associates, Architects and Planners.

Mrs Demers, Social Development Officer, Washington New Town.

Mr Norman Dennis, Department of Social Studies, University of Newcastle upon Tyne.

Mr G. R. Dixon, Culham College, Berkshire.

Professor David Donnison, Department of Social Science and Social Administration, London School of Economics.

Mr A. H. Ensor, Newland Park College, Bucks.

Mr D. J. Escott, City of Portsmouth College of Education.

Mr George Evans, Chief Welfare Officer, Cheshire County Council.

Miss Joan Eyden, Department of Applied Social Science, University of Nottingham.

Miss Elsie Fisher, Park Centre, Burgess Hill.

Mr E. J. Gardiner, Association of Municipal Corporations.

Miss Dulcie Groves, Kingston College of Technology.

Professor Arnold Gurin, Brandeis University, Massachusetts.

Mr Robin Guthrie, Cambridge House Settlement, London.

Mr Keith Hill, Manchester University Settlement.

Dr H. M. Holden, The Tavistock Institute of Human Relations, London.

Mr W. L. Hooper, Greater London Council.

Mr R. Huws Jones, National Institute for Social Work Training, London.

Mr Nelson C. Jackson, National Association of Social Workers, New York.

Mr W. G. Jackson, City of Nottingham Education Committee.

Professor Marie Jahoda, School of Psychology, University of Sussex.

Professor Elliott Jaques, School of Social Sciences, Brunel University.

Mr S. Jones, Chingford Community Association.

Mr Tecwin Jones, Toxteth Community Council, Liverpool.

Dr Israel Katz, Paul Baerwald School of Social Work, The Hebrew University, Jerusalem.

Professor Bryan Keith-Lucas, Department of Political Studies, University of Kent.

Dr Josephine Klein, School of Educational Studies, University of Sussex.

Mr Peter Kuenstler, United Nations, Geneva.

Mr Peter Leonard, National Institute for Social Work Training, London.

Miss M. Lewis, British Association of Residential Settlements.

Dr Kenneth Little, Department of Social Anthropology, University of Edinburgh.

Mr J. A. Mack, School of Social Study, University of Glasgow.

Professor W. J. M. Mackenzie, Department of Politics, University of Glasgow.

The late Professor Samuel Mencher, University of Pittsburgh.

Mr P. K. C. Millins, Edgehill College, Ormskirk.

The Revd. Dr F. Milson, Westhill College of Education, Birmingham.

Mr John Moulton, Community Worker, Swindon.

Mr R. Mullelly, Cumberland Council of Social Service.

Dr Roy Parker, Department of Social Science and Social Administration, London School of Economics.

Mr J. Parr, Westhill College of Education, Birmingham.

Miss Nadine Peppard, National Committee for Commonwealth Immigrants.

Professor Robert Perlman, Council on Social Work Education, Community Organization Curriculum Development Project, Brandeis University, Massachusetts.

Mr G. Plowman, Department of Social Science and Social Administration, London School of Economics.

Mr H. R. Poole, Liverpool Council of Social Service.

Mr G. Popplestone, Department of Sociology, University of Aberdeen.

Mr P. Rathbone, Institute of Town Planning.

Dr Martin Rein, School of Social Work, Bryn Mawr College, Pennsylvania.

Mr M. Reinold, National Federation of Community Associations.

Dr R. Revans, Association Européenne des Centres de Perfectionnement dans la Direction des Entreprises, Brussels.

Mr G. Riches, London Council of Social Service.

Mr K. W. Robbins, Town Clerk's Department, Harringey.

Miss B. H. Roberts, Talbot House Settlement, London.

Miss E. Roché, Nottingham Council of Social Service.

Professor Bernard Ross, School of Social Work, Bryn Mawr College, Pennsylvania.

Professor Jack Rothman, School of Social Work, University of Michigan.

Mr A. N. Scarrott, Gloucestershire Community Council.

Dr Meyer Schwartz, School of Social Work, University of Pittsburgh.

Mr J. E. Simmonds, School of Educational Studies, University of Sussex.

Professor S. Slavin, School of Social Work, Columbia University, New York.

Miss M. R. Smith, Swansea College of Education.

Dr John Spencer, Department of Social Study, University of Edinburgh.

Mr Simon Spiro, Paul Baerwald School of Social Work, The Hebrew University, Jerusalem.

Sister St John, S.N.D., Notre Dame College of Education, Liverpool.

Mrs Margaret Stacey, Department of Sociology and Anthropology, University College, Swansea.

Professor Paul Stirling, Department of Sociology, University of Kent.

Mr B. K. Taylor, Department of Social Administration, University College, Swansea.

Miss Margery Taylor, London Boroughs Training Committee.

Dr G. Thomason, Department of Industrial Relations, University College, Cardiff.

Professor Richard Titmuss, Department of Social Science and Social Administration, London School of Economics.

Mr J. Vaughan Williams, Risca Adult Education Centre, South Wales.

Miss P. Warren, Camden Council of Social Service.

Mr Len White, Liaison Officer, Harlow Development Corporation.

Mr P. Williams, Sussex Rural Community Council.

Miss D. Wilson, Bishop Creighton House Settlement, London.

Appendix B

Community Development and Community Organisation

The following brief notes about community development and community organisation in other parts of the world supplement what was said in chapter 2 (p. 11) about the contribution which these can make to advances in this country through a growing body of theory underlying practice.

COMMUNITY DEVELOPMENT

Community development is mainly associated with the problems of rural people in underdeveloped areas. Its purposes are to help people to improve their economic and material conditions and to rouse them from the apathy and fatalism of the centuries. In the 1940s community development began to emerge as a method for speeding up national development, particularly in Asia and Africa.[1] In previous decades, notably in India in the 1930s, early isolated projects, sponsored by the missions and talented individuals, evolved a field practice which later influenced programmes of community development from the 1940s. These programmes were a response to a new situation differentiated from the prewar period by rapid change and by growth in the social and economic ambitions of national governments. The administrators and planners were no longer talking in terms of gradual progress over a hundred years. Target dates were reduced to twenty, ten, five, or even fewer years and development planning had to adjust as best it could.

Two factors emerged from this period of change and adjustment which can be said to have been largely responsible for the growth of community development as a field of professional work:

1. Old forms of government and the fixed traditions of extended family and tribal patterns which had sufficed with little change in stable situations were incapable of dealing with the need for accelerated development. Thus development teams made up of specialist officers were created to promote and guide change. New appointments were made, such as development commissioners, with wide ranging terms of reference, outside the traditional hierarchy of administration.
2. In order to achieve the rate of social and economic development that was required it began to be realised that the people must be

1. See, for example, *Mass Education in African Society*, H.M.S.O., 1944.

educated and motivated to take some responsibility for bringing about change and achieving development goals; for example, improved nutrition, agricultural methods or sanitation could not be attained where traditional methods and superstititions had persisted for generations.

In time there grew up a body of principles and practice which became characteristic of community development work in many countries. But it must be remembered that the practice came first and the principles followed as a result of trial and error, which sometimes led to success and sometimes failure. Amongst the various concepts associated with community development are 'felt needs', 'self help', 'local initiative' and 'a holistic approach'. With the exception of the last named, all these terms refer to the desirability of an educative and reciprocal relationship between development, administration and local people, and the importance of involving them in decision making and implementation processes.

The United Nations has made considerable and varied contributions to community development, including the often quoted definition:

1. The term community development has come into international usage to connote the processes by which the efforts of the people themselves are united with those of governmental authorities to improve the economic, social and cultural conditions of communities, to integrate these communities into the life of the nation, and to enable them to contribute fully to national progress.
2. This complex of processes is, then, made up of two essential elements: the participation by the people themselves in efforts to improve their level of living with as much reliance as possible on their own initiative; and the provision of technical and other services in ways which encourage initiative, self help and mutual aid and make these more effective. It is expressed in programmes designed to achieve a wide variety of specific improvements.[1]

Because community development has located the real focus in the need to motivate people to bring about attitude changes which will remedy deficiencies in knowledge, in confidence and in skills, rather than in the unexploited, or underexploited, natural resources of these countries, it has been compelled to advocate methods which are slower to produce results than is the application of sophisticated technology to physical problems. Consequently it has been

1. United Nations, *Report on Concepts and Principles of Community Development*, Annex 2, 1956, pp. 1–2.

frequently, though incorrectly, assumed that community development is concerned primarily with process goals, or the quality of life, rather than with task goals, the achievement of concrete objectives.

Community development workers are primarily employed to precipitate and guide change. Much of their work has been centred on problems of resistance to change, and the attempt to accommodate new ways within some existing cultural assumptions. Community development is thus concerned with conserving the social fabric as well as with innovation. Although it has been mainly undertaken in rural areas, the rapid growth of shanty towns in most developing countries, with all their problems of rootlessness, unemployment, prostitution, delinquency and loss of family and kinship ties, began to focus attention belatedly on the need for large-scale urban community development and planning.

COMMUNITY ORGANISATION IN THE UNITED STATES

Community work covers a very broad and diverse range of activities in the United States. These have been variously called community organisation, community development, neighbourhood organisation, community or social action, health and welfare planning, and social planning. The centre of gravity of these activities, traditionally identified as 'community organisation', evolved from the charity organisation societies and the settlement movement at the turn of the century and the councils of social agencies or welfare councils which a few decades later grew out of projects for joint fund-raising and coordination of voluntary social agencies.

From the beginning, therefore, practice and training in community organisation have been associated with the growth of social work as a profession within the field of social welfare. Community organisation followed casework and group work as the third and most recent specialisation in schools of social work in the universities.

Not surprisingly, quite different interpretations of community organisation have evolved in different situations. Thus Marris and Rein writing on anti-poverty campaigns in the U.S.A. list at least seven different types of processes to which the label community organisation had been attached:

1. the process of helping the local community to adapt to the pressures of external forces, deriving perhaps from new legislation or economic changes, affecting its neighbourhood;
2. the provision of assistance in the way of social therapy to combat the effects of social disintegration;
3. the provision of schemes for leadership training and forms of vocational training for people who are otherwise unemployable;

4. a process of development administration in which the needs of the people concerned are taken into account in planning activities;
5. a process by which people might be educated to participate more fully in democratic government;
6. a means by which new types of community might be evolved to perform some of the needed functions, such as integration, once performed by the now displaced traditional closed community;
7. a process which would create new sources of power within the social system to press for reform.[1]

There are also distinctions in the analytic position of community organisation theorists; for example, Murray Ross defines community organisation as 'a process by which a community identifies its needs or objectives, orders (or ranks) these needs or objectives, develops the confidence and will to work at these needs or objectives, finds the resources (internal and/or external) to deal with these needs or objectives, takes action in respect to them and in so doing extends and develops cooperative and collaborative attitudes and practices in the community'.[2] This definition leans heavily upon group problem solving theory, which is an important element in community work but the definition assumes group agreement rather than conflicting demands and it ignores problems of scarce resources. It is also mainly concerned with grass roots community development rather than community organisation at the inter-agency and planning levels.

1. Marris and Rein, *Dilemmas of Social Reform: Poverty and Community Action in the United States*, Routledge & Kegan Paul, 1967, pp. 168–9.
2. Murray G. Ross with B. W. Lappin, *Community Organisation: Theory, Principles and Practice*, second edition, Harper & Row, 1967, p. 40.

Appendix C

Examples of Numbers and Qualifications of Existing Community Workers and of Appointments

EXAMPLES OF COMMUNITY WORKERS (NUMBERS, BACKGROUND AND QUALIFICATIONS)

Community centre wardens (information supplied by the National Federation of Community Associations, July 1967)

Background and training (250 wardens)	*Percentage of all wardens*
Trained teachers	4
Westhill course	4
Trained youth leaders	20 (steadily increasing)
Other qualifications (e.g. degree, social science diploma, Y.M.C.A. training)	22
Direct recruits from industry, voluntary social work, etc.	50
	100

All community centre wardens are eligible for membership of the Community Service Association, which has the following objectives:

To further the interest of professional workers in community associations and centres, settlements and kindred organisations which exist to promote the well being of communities through social, recreational, physical and educational activities, and to assist the development and efficiency of the work undertaken by them.

The National Federation of Community Associations, an associated group of the National Council of Social Service, promotes and coordinates the work of community associations and centres.

Residential settlements (information supplied by the British Association of Residential Settlements, July 1967)

Background and training of wardens (13 replies)	*Percentage*
Degree in social science	17
Social studies diploma or similar	

159

training	15
Degree and diploma in education	6
Minister of religion	6
Youth leadership training	20
Others	36
	100

In the majority of cases recruitment was from related social work fields, but six wardens had previous experience in the forces or the civil service. The British Association of Residential Settlements acts as a link between the affiliated settlements. Some settlements are not affiliated. In addition there are links with the Educational Centres Association.

Secretaries of councils of social service (information supplied by
the National Council of Social Service, July 1967)

Background and training	*Percentage*
(71 replies)	
Degree but no professional training	16
Social studies qualification	33
Relevant further education or academic training	6
No academic or relevant training	45
	100

Assistant secretaries in councils of social service

Background and training	*Percentage*
(28 replies)	
Degree but no professional qualification	10
Social studies qualification	29
Relevant further education or academic training	3
No academic or relevant training	58
	100

Secretaries of rural community councils

Background and training (42 replies)	Percentage
Forces	17
Colonial service	14
Local government	19
Directly relevant experience	29
Business and industry	5
Not known	16
	100

Twelve of the secretaries of rural community councils were promoted from the field and a few started their career in this work. The National Council of Social Service coordinates the work of the separate councils and assists in the promotion of new ones.

Community relations officers (information supplied by the National Committee for Commonwealth Immigrants, 1968)
There are thirty-eight officers. Their previous experience included teaching, social work, personnel management and the police force.

Social development officers (information supplied by the Ministry of Housing and Local Government, 1967)
The Ministry is in touch with seventeen chief and thirty-four assistant social development officers in new towns, the majority of whom are graduates.

SALARY SCALES AND QUALIFICATIONS

Post	Salary range	Scale	Qualifications
Community centre wardens	1. Qualified £825–1290 (scale) (with additional responsibility allowance up to £450)	Joint Negotiating Committee for Youth Leaders and Community Centre Wardens	1. Trained youth leader 2. Westhill College of Education
			3. Five years' experience in post
	2. Unqualified £620–825 (scale)	ditto	None laid down
Wardens of residential settlements	1. Qualified £1725–2105 (recommended)	ditto	ditto
	2. Unqualified £820–1020 minimum	ditto	ditto

Post	Salary range	Scale	Qualifications
Secretaries of local councils of social service	£1385–1875 (scale A) or £1170–1620 (scale B)	National Council of Social Service ditto	None laid down ditto
Assistant C.S.S. secretaries	£1005–1405 (scale A) or £860–1340 (scale B)	ditto	ditto
Secretaries of rural community councils	1. £1457–2137 2. £1328–1842 3. £1243–1639	Civil service executive grade	ditto ditto ditto
Assistant R.C.C. secretaries	Approximately as for assistant C.S.S. secretaries	National Council of Social Service	ditto
Unattached neighbour-hood workers	£900–1700	Burnham Scale B (some appointments)	ditto
Community development officers	£1180–1500	A.P.T. scales	ditto
Community relations officers	£1200–2006 (range)	None	ditto
New towns social development officers	£2000–3000 (range)	Whitley Council for new towns' staff	ditto
Assistant social development officers	£1000–1800 (range)	A.P.T. scales	ditto
Headquarters staff in some national organisations	£1850–2700 (scale) (N.C.S.S.)	Related to civil service administrative grades	ditto
University lecturers in aspects of community work	£1470–2630	University scale	Relevant degree and experience

N.B. Most posts have pension benefits and car allowances. Advertisements may specify the qualifications desirable. There does not appear to be either a bar to promotion or a salary bar for those without such qualifications.

DESCRIPTION OF SOME EXISTING POSTS

The descriptions which follow illustrate from advertisements or job descriptions some recently created posts.

Neighbourhood worker in new housing area (local authority)
1. To meet all newcomers and to deal with any immediate problems they have.
2. To stimulate the emergence of social groups.
3. To refer family casework to the appropriate agencies.
4. To act as liaison between the local authority and the tenants.
5. To report as may be required to the appropriate committee.
   (Salary scale A.P.T. 2 or 3.) Responsible to the Town Clerk.

City of Edinburgh, centre coordinator for experimental health and welfare advice centre
The project, an important extension in the field of community care, is sited in the City, which at present draws heavily on all existing services. The coordinator will be responsible for liaison with the statutory and voluntary agencies and will have every opportunity to plan and administer the project. Imagination and administrative ability and interest in research and wide experience as a practising social worker will be needed for this challenging post.

Haleward Community Council, community development officer
Appointed to this parish in a rural district of Lancashire which is being developed by the Liverpool Corporation for the rehousing of slum clearance areas and overspill. The job analysis gives the usual description of the functions of the development officer in a scheme which includes leasing an old school house to provide an operational base and a flat for the officer concerned. Reference is made to the supervision of students and the use of community service volunteers.

Community services assistant (local authority)
1. To raise to a higher level the work of community development at present being undertaken.
2. To cooperate with and encourage coordination of statutory and voluntary welfare bodies.
3. To assist in the planning of social provision required in further expansion of the borough.

Assistant town clerk
1. To coordinate and integrate more closely the work of existing departments so as to achieve the greatest possible cooperation, particularly in programming new projects, in joint service arrangements and in improvements in existing services.

163

2. To have special responsibility for integrating the welfare, health, children's and housing services.

City of Birmingham Housing Management Department, social development officer

A new appointment concerned with the sociological aspects of large-scale development of new and old areas. Duties include social planning, community development, liaison with statutory and voluntary organisations, research into population trends, public relations and the issuing of information and advice. The holder will play a vital part in the successful development of new housing estates, major redevelopment schemes and the clearance of large areas.

Scotland, Chief Adviser on Social Work

Civil Service post created in connection with the reorganisation of local authority social work services foreshadowed in the Scottish White Paper. The departmental professional advisers concerned with welfare, child care and probation and approved school services, have recently been formed, together with related administrative officers, into an integrated Social Work Services Group. The chief adviser will take charge of the professional element of this group. He will be expected to advise and assist in the professional aspects of reorganisation of the local authority social work services and also to make a positive contribution to the development of social aspects of policy on other matters for which the Secretary of State is responsible, e.g. education, housing and planning.

Notes on the kind of experience and qualifications which will be useful were added to the job description but there was no absolute requirement except 'an ability to plan, organise and develop the services in question and to work with professional and administrative officers at both national and local levels'.

Newcastle upon Tyne, conservation officer (City Planning Department)

A local conservation officer for one part of the City as a sort of intermediary between the citizens and the Corporation's Planning Department. A newspaper cutting states that his job combines the roles of 'council watchdog and people's friend'.

The Research Section of the Planning Department is responsible for plotting on City maps all aspects of social malaise and coding these for mechanical analysis, in order to investigate the relationships between aspects of social ill-health and housing and environmental conditions. A regular meeting of officers from various departments takes place and is chaired by the medical officer of health.

*National Institute for Social Work Training, senior fieldworker and
supervisor to a five-year community project in Southwark*
He will be responsible for developing the work of a small team of
community workers and for working closely with local residents and
organisations, both statutory and voluntary. He should be able to
analyse the work of the project and present it to others, to prepare
the field for student training and to teach in the Institute's training
programme.

*Yorkshire, West Riding, principal responsible for further education
in an area (seventeen such appointments)*
The principal helps to promote the integration of the various agencies
for further education in the area and to establish liaison with local
employers, voluntary organisations and other bodies. Most of those
appointed to these posts have had experience in evening institutes,
community centre work or the youth service. The primary need is a
capacity to establish fruitful relationships, together with imagination
and vigour.

A new town social relations officer
The social relations officer is responsible to the General Manager
and the Corporation as a Chief Officer. Functions include:
1. *Research.* Assembly and analysis of relevant statistics from other
   new towns, etc., helpful in predicting future trends – in population,
   accommodation, requirements, shopping, industry, recreation
   and open space; social surveys in the area, including liaison with
   university departments; collection of statistics on incoming
   population for submission to the Ministry of Housing and Local
   Government and also for own use in adjusting earlier projections,
   in particular of population growth and accommodation needs;
   provision of statistics for other departments.
2. *Information* to general public and relations with local and national
   press; organisation of exhibitions (in collaboration with the Chief
   Architect Planner); arrangements for visitors and tours of the
   area; preparation of leaflets and booklets.
3. *Community development.* The production of a social programme
   on which plans are based. The Department produces for the Chief
   Architect Planner a brief for each area of the town on which the
   physical plan is based. This brief sets out: (*a*) the accommodation
   structure (in consultation with the Chief Estates Officer); (*b*)
   social facilities including community buildings, children's play
   facilities, child welfare clinics, doctors' and dentists' surgeries,
   libraries and schools; (*c*) open space requirements.

Initial operation and management of local community centres and
supervised children's playgrounds (until local authority is able to

take over responsibility). Guidance of bodies administering large-scale district or central social and sports facilities; general support and encouragement to formation of social groups in the area.

He is the primary Corporation contact with the County Medical Officer of Health, the County Education Officer, the County Welfare Officer, the County Librarian, and is the Corporation's representative on the Council of Social Service; the county Playing Fields Association; the New Towns Society; the regional Sports Council; the local Arts Council; the Town and Country Planning Association.

Appendix D

Specimen Syllabus for a Course on Principles and Methods of Community Work

A SURVEY OF COMMUNITY WORK

A general analytic description of community work and its varieties; the past history, present state and possible future development of community work; the organisations and people engaged in it; the relation of community work to other forms of professional and administrative activity; community work in relation to social policy and social welfare.

THE NATURE OF COMMUNITY WORK

Community work methods and the role of the community worker, leading to a broad formulation of community work practice along the lines already described. The aim would be to develop a framework for understanding and practising community work which could be elaborated, modified and applied in detailed study of community work practice.

THE SOCIAL CONTEXT OF COMMUNITY WORK

The community worker must be familiar with social science concepts relevant to community work practice, especially the structure, functions and processes of the community and the nature of social problems. Certain social science concepts would need to be applied and illustrated whether or not the students had had – or were having – background social science courses.

PRINCIPLES OF COMMUNITY WORK

The values, assumptions, attitudes and purposes of community work, for example, as set out in chapters 3, 6, 7 and 9.

THE AUSPICES OF COMMUNITY WORK

The functions, policies and practices of organisations undertaking community work, and the implications of these for the purposes and tasks of the work on the lines of the discussions in chapters 6 and 7. The worker must understand the effects of the organisational structure within which he works and his own position in it, as well as the operations of other organisations which will impinge on his work or whose aid he may need.

COMMUNITY WORK METHODS

These should be considered under two headings:

Analysis: observation, fact-finding, study, assessment, analysis and planning as part of the community work process.
Interaction: forming and sustaining relationships, working with individuals, groups, organisations, representatives and committees as part of the community work process.

The application of these two methods will require discussion in a number of specific situations, bringing in also illustrations from the students' field experience in relation to:

Work with community groups: the processes of work with groups, whether neighbourhood or special interest groups or both, to enable them to articulate their needs and to take appropriate collective action about them.
Inter-organisation work: the processes of cooperation, coordination and joint planning between organisations operating in the field of social welfare in order to strengthen, modify and develop their activities so as to meet the social needs of the community more adequately.

THE COMMUNITY WORK OF THE PERSONAL SERVICE AGENCY

Organisations providing personal services to individuals, families or groups must engage in community work in order to fulfil their direct service responsibilities to clients more adequately. Three interrelated areas of activity can be distinguished. First, the mobilisation of resources – the process of obtaining funds, personnel, facilities, clients, authority, understanding, support and so on, necessary to maintain and develop the service.

Second, the development of relationships with other agencies who can help or hinder the carrying out of the tasks of the service.

Third, bringing about changes in the quality and quantity of community resources necessary to provide adequate service to people in a neighbourhood or to clients with particular needs.

SOCIAL PLANNING

Community work at the level of social planning is an activity that concerns itself with proposals for the future, with evaluation of alternative proposals, and with methods by which these proposals might be achieved. As such it is primarily analytical but even in this respect it requires contact with those who are involved in various ways in order to obtain information, determine priorities, anticipate reactions and so on. Increasingly, however, social planning is taken to include not only proposals for future action but also the process of implementing the proposals and of evaluating the results so that interaction becomes as important as analysis and each activity sustains the other. Social planning seeks to alter social conditions and deal with social problems by changing the policies, responsibilities, resources and relationships of formal organisations.

At this stage community work is concerned with the planning of social welfare, and with the social welfare aspects of other activities such as housing, employment and education, rather than with social planning in the fullest sense. As such it has much in common with inter-organisational work but may be distinguished in terms of level of organisation to be modified.

SPECIFIC SKILLS OF COMMUNITY WORK

A variety of specific skills enter into community work and it would be beyond the scope of any course to provide students with all the skills and techniques which might at some time or other be useful. It must also be remembered that none of these skills will ever be perfectly achieved. The crucial question is how much of each of them in combination with the others is required for effective community work of different kinds. Skills are needed in the following:

Interpersonal relations
Students need to know how to establish and maintain effective contacts with people, both as individuals and as members of formal or informal groups.

Group relations
The formation and support of groups of all kinds – from the most informal through to committees and councils – for a wide variety of purposes and helping such groups to participate and to work effectively at their tasks is clearly a basic skill of community work.

Education and training is a major element in much community work. Usually it is very informal, using problems and situations actually encountered as a means of developing greater understanding and competence on the part of both the participants and the community worker. It will also include more structured training events and training courses when appropriate. The community worker has a continuing responsibility for recruiting and training volunteers. He must be fully aware of the crucial importance of voluntary effort in community work, the growth of local leadership and continuing support for local groups. He may also have responsibility for the in-service training, staff development and supervision of paid staff.

Fact-finding and social investigation

Collecting and analysing information relevant to the tasks in hand is an important aspect of the community worker's job and an essential element in his training. It includes the understanding and use of statistical data.

Communication

The community worker needs skills in communication, in adult education techniques and in public relations to establish effective contact in order to enlighten people about problems, policies, procedures and services; to gain support for activities and developments; to encourage participation and the use of opportunities and facilities. Written and verbal communication in the form of articles, press releases, leaflets, reports, speaking, public meetings, conferences, etc., are the most usual methods but the use of audio-visual aids, including radio, television and films is increasingly important.

Administration

The community worker needs some understanding of the principles of management and some skill in the techniques of organisation and administration. He will usually be a member of an organisation whose working he needs to understand if he is to be effective; he will be working closely with a variety of other organisations whose cooperation will be vital to his work; and he will often carry various administrative and organisational responsibilities including responsibility for other staff.

Finance and budgeting.

Community work often requires the preparation of budgets for the implementation of proposals, special projects, extensions of services, running of services, etc., and the community worker may often play a part in fund raising from statutory sources, voluntary giving, foundations, etc.

Recording.

Recording is an essential tool of the community worker. It is used for a variety of purposes – research, fact-finding and analysis, information, public relations, social action, administration, assessment, and the development of understanding and skill in community work. The community worker needs the ability to devise appropriate records and to use his own and other people's records.

170

THE INTERRELATION OF SKILLS

These specific skills or techniques are interrelated and overlapping. Many aspects of the total content of training contribute to them and they are implicit in the analytical and interactional tasks of the community worker. Analytical skills can to a considerable extent be practised in the classroom. Theoretical study can provide some understanding of interactional skills and they can to some extent be simulated in the classroom or experienced through group interaction but real ability in group relationships can only grow through guided and analysed practical experience. It is assumed that a course such as the foregoing would be taught in close relation to fieldwork so that students begin to see the relevance in real life of what they are discussing in the classroom, and conversely field experience is used to give greater precision and depth to theory.